SimpleSpaces

SimpleSpaces, Inc
1442 E. 820 N. Orem, UT 84097
Ph. 801.225.1153
www.simplespacesinc.com

Published by:
Digital Legend, Rochester, NY 2007
ISBN-13: 978-1-934537-75-6
ISBN-10: 1-934537-75-6

For Mom and Dad,
who have always given me space.

■   ■   ■   ■

For Chris and
Rachel, Jesse, Christopher, Michael,
Sarah, Braden, Eliza, Hannah, Mark,
and Jonathan.

SimpleSpaces

Is there a space that I can find
truth in my heart and in my mind?

I've looked above, I've looked below;
is there a place that I can go?

A quiet place, a space serene,
I'll look inside to find my dream.

If I can read and choose to learn,
I'll walk this path; now is my turn.

Opening the door, you enter the space. Standing in the threshold of the room, you see order. You breathe easily as your eyes move from area to area. There are shapes, colors, and pieces residing together in a pattern you have created. There is harmony here. You continue further into the room, returning to their places the things you have carried with you. You decide to sit. As your gaze falls on an object, you are pleasantly reminded of why it is here with you. Further over, you see an empty surface, and your eyes linger there. In the quiet, you remember an important task that needs to be done. Again, you breathe in and out peacefully. This is home.

This is your space.

There is a stream of sunlight on the far wall, falling onto the floor. You imagine stretching out in its path, feeling the warmth of the sun directly. Across the room a plant grows, alive and vibrant; it has flourished in this area. You feel grateful for this place. You can relax here. You can listen, making peace with your thoughts, choosing and creating new ones. You calmly prepare for your next endeavor.

A moment of serenity has enveloped you, and you feel content with your world.

What are SimpleSpaces? Spaces that are free . . . free from holding to the past or predicting the future, spaces that serve the present day and all that is required to fulfill it.

A SimpleSpace is one that you create; it is the birth and sustaining of a place you call home. Your living happens here. You interact with others, sharing time in this space. Here you feed your body and care for it daily. You feed your mind here with thoughts, words, and images of your choosing. You feel in this space, experiencing pain, excitement, anger, and joy. SimpleSpaces are areas you have, and will yet create, where you are free to be who you are and who you dream of becoming. Because the energy is vital in these spaces, you have the strength and courage to forge bonds with friends and family, to heal past wounds and forgive offenses.

SimpleSpaces give you time to care for what is necessary and important, leaving alone what is wasteful and unproductive. These spaces allow you to listen and know what truth is.

If you fear time to think, you may not easily embrace SimpleSpaces because time is what you naturally will be given. As your spaces become ordered and free, you will find order and experience freedom. You will grow in self-awareness and knowledge by virtue of the peace and harmony surrounding you. This self-awareness can be frightening at times, but it is always familiar and ultimately safe.

You already know who you really are.

There are 4 Steps used to create SimpleSpaces. These Steps are natural, like breathing. Learning to recognize and utilize them will effect great changes in your spaces, those outside of you and inside, physical and emotional. As you walk this path, you will learn to change these places forever.

If the 4 Steps are fulfilled in patience, you will always experience the same result: serenity. You will enjoy this serenity for a time, until you cannot, and then you will walk the path again. You will create SimpleSpaces again and again.

We are born with nothing, and we die with none of our earthly possessions, only the knowledge we have acquired. We arrive on this earth unclothed and empty-handed, and we leave in the same manner. What we do in the space between that entrance and exit is our life's journey. All that we receive, purchase, consume, handle, and call our own, facilitate this life. Knowing what is truly necessary and sacred is imperative: what to hold onto, share with someone else, or throw away. When we free-up our spaces of all that isn't vital, we free ourselves from the responsibility and concern for those things.

As we simplify our spaces . . . we free-up our lives, literally.

You have already experienced the 4 Steps in your everyday living. Now you can read and learn what they are, becoming aware of their potential impact on your life.

May you create spaces that support your journey.

May you create SimpleSpaces . . . again and again.

Step 1
evaluate

Step 2
eliminate

Step 3
employ

Step 4
enjoy

■　　　■　　　■　　　■

Step 1

evaluate

evaluate

yellow increases mental clarity

evaluate

evaluate

yellow clears a foggy head

yellow stimulates the intellect

yellow increases mental clarity

evaluate

Step 1

e v a l u a t e

I will be honest with all that I see and hear.
I do not fear the truth.

Step 1

In the quiet of my heart can be heard all the answers.
As I have sought, I have found. As I have asked, I have been given.

observe and ask

listen and receive

record and verify

visualize and dream

■　　■　　■　　■

Step 1

observe and ask

Now you begin Step 1.

This is a time for evaluating. Take time to observe.

In a quiet moment, begin this phase. Be alone. It will be best for you to begin this Step during the day when the light of the sun can be seen and felt in each room. It need not be a sunny day; even light through the clouds will illuminate what you will see. If it is raining, recognize the lack of light you will experience and continue.

Begin this Step in a space that is most in need of simplifying.

You may choose any area.

You should use the 4 Steps of SimpleSpaces for each individual area. Select a space, and walk through all 4 Steps within that place. This will allow you to focus clearly. You may be overwhelmed if you apply the 4 Steps to multiple spaces simultaneously.

By choosing one specific area, your energy will remain focused. Eventually, you will create SimpleSpaces in all the areas you call home. This cannot be accomplished in one day, but will transpire over time, at a pace you will determine. When a SimpleSpace has been completed, you will naturally move into the next area that needs this process.

Think of the spaces that exist. Each of these can be transformed. These may include: entryways, kitchens, bedrooms, bathrooms, living rooms, dens, playrooms, closets, pantries, attics, basements, laundry rooms, offices, storage rooms, and any other spaces you own. You will want to include garages, sheds, or any adjacent buildings. This may seem daunting as you consider all the spaces you occupy. Remember, it has taken time to create these places, and it will take time to transform them. If fulfilled in patience, the 4 Steps will change these areas dramatically.

As you simplify your spaces . . . you will free-up your life.

This process of simplifying will be yours to use over and over again. You will become proficient at taking these Steps. As you proceed, temper your eagerness with patience: read, learn, and begin. These spaces and their contents have been a part of your journey. They will continue to influence who you are and who you will become. These Steps are crucial; SimpleSpaces cannot be realized without them.

Again, choose to begin in a space that feels most in need of simplifying.

You will use your eyes to observe. If you do not have the gift of sight, use other senses that will allow you to evaluate and feel the energy of this place.

You are beginning the evaluation Step. As you proceed, you will recognize its importance.

■   ■   ■   ■

Now enter the space you have chosen. Be alert and aware. Position yourself in the threshold of the room, and look at all that is around you. Leave no areas unobserved. See the colors, shapes, and objects that live in this space. When you have observed all that is within your view, venture further inside. Look into containers, and see what is being stored. Look behind things, under pieces, and into corners. Let your eyes travel up the walls and down to the floor. Notice the light, or lack of light, in this space. Observe the variety and textures of the materials here: fabrics, plastics, metals, and woods. Are things soft or hard, round or square, inanimate or alive? Notice the condition of the objects in this place. Observe what is old, new, familiar, strange, peeling, torn, shiny, dusty, purposeful, or unnecessary. Do not hurry as you do this, or think of other spaces yet to be evaluated. Concentrate on this room and be aware. Simply be there.

Observe objects that reside in this space, and think of where they came from; recall their history and how they came to be here. Stories likely will fill your mind, and your thoughts will travel to other times and places as you become reacquainted with each object.

Allow yourself to remember.

Emotions will follow in the wake of thoughts. You will feel these emotions if you allow yourself. And time will pass as you carry out this observation phase.

■   ■   ■   ■

Feel gratitude for the opportunity to be where you are, for all that rests in this space.

These objects are wholly or partially, if shared with another, your stewardship. Recognize your ownership. Think about this responsibility. There is a mantle of power bestowed on the owner of the things in this space enabling that person to decide if, when, or where these things will reside. Only you know, as you stand in this room, what belongs to you. Do not own what you know is not yours, but honestly observe and evaluate what is. Remember, you own these objects; they do not own you.

Take a breath and exhale. You are in every way observing what is before you.

When you see the same things again and experience recurring thoughts about those things, you are nearing the end of observation. You will feel as if you are hearing a familiar song, and you will recognize the melody as it begins. When you continue to look into this space, and gain no new insights about what you are seeing, you will know that you have spent sufficient time observing.

Now it is time to ask. Remain in the room. Look back over the areas you have observed. Now you will begin to ask.

Asking questions is a method you will use to gain knowledge. Now that you have evaluated by observing, you are going to evaluate by asking. As you formulate questions in your mind and send them into the space, be prepared to receive answers. These answers will give you important insights.

Remember, when we ask questions, we must understand within ourselves that we will receive answers. Understanding this can be uncomfortable if we are not prepared to receive. But no one wants to ask questions that have no answers. As night follows day, so answers follow questions if we wait to receive them.

If you are willing to ask, you must also be willing to receive.

Some people ask questions to which they do not want to hear the answers. Other people ask questions to which they already know the answers, and their questions are superficial. Sometimes we are unsure of the answers we have been given, and we ask again to receive verification. This can be a necessary action. When a question is asked of another, that person will use time and energy formulating an answer. Appreciate the effort that an answer requires.

When we ask sincerely, we will receive truthfully.

■   ■   ■   ■

As you stand in this space, pause to reflect on the power and efficacy of questions and answers. Feel gratitude for the ability you have to participate in this 4 Step process. You have the opportunity to evaluate this space.

Gratitude is an expression of appreciation. Being grateful allows you to acknowledge all that is pleasing and positive in your life. You can even be grateful for challenges and struggles. Gratitude brings feelings of happiness and contentment, and opens your heart to positive energy. If positive energy resides in your heart, that energy will be felt in the space.

When you feel gratitude, it will be reflected in your spaces.

This is a powerful reality. You will fulfill the 4 Steps more effectively if you can feel gratitude along the way.

Now in this room you will ask questions that will allow you to learn truths you did not know. You will send your questions into the space, directing them towards particular objects, shapes, and pieces. As you question, you will allow the objects residing to defend their right to be there. You will do this to affirm that the things you have chosen to live with are necessary for your journey. You may feel foolish standing alone in the space, conversing with inanimate objects, but there is a life force that exists even in material things.

There is energy in this place.

This process of asking is necessary because of the truths you will receive concerning all that resides here. Trust this part of the process. Your questions may begin like this: "What is the purpose of this room?" "What do I do in this place?" "Why is that here?" "Who gave it to me?" "When do I use this?" "Where did it come from?"

Other questions to ask of your space that are more introspective include: "Do I love that?" "Do I feel I owe something to it?" "Could I live without that?"

Questioning further you may ask: "Does someone need this more than I do?"

Remember, ask as many questions as you need, to understand the truth that exists in this place. If you ask general questions, you will receive general answers. If you take the time and thought to ask specific questions, you will receive specific answers.

The most vital question of all: "How do I feel in this space?" "How do I feel when I look in that drawer, inside that closet, or underneath that piece of furniture?" Ask, and then open your mind to the answers that will come.

Having observed, you are now willing to look more closely and ask.

This process takes time.

SimpleSpaces take time.

This will take time away from other activities in which you would normally be engaged. This will require energy of mind and heart.

Now that you have observed and asked, you will wait.

Wait for answers.

Step 1

I now see and question.

observe and ask

Step 1

evaluate

observe and ask

listen and receive

record and verify

visualize and dream

■   ■   ■   ■

Step 1

listen and receive

Remain inside the space to continue this phase of evaluation.

You will listen and receive.

Make sure you are still alone and free from distraction; the phone is turned down, and things are quiet. You must not be interrupted. You may stand or sit. Listening and receiving requires that you be comfortable and focused, calm and unperturbed. This phase will flow naturally from observing and asking. You will begin by listening.

You are listening for answers to the questions you have asked.

It is important to recognize this stage of evaluation. Now that you have asked, it is critical that you wait and listen. Listening is a simple thing if we know how. It takes awareness and energy.

You must be attentive and focused to listen. It is an action. In the stillness and quiet of your space, you will hear.

Listening is accomplished with the ears, but hearing the truth is understood in the mind and felt in the heart. If you are alone, the information you receive will come from within and through you. There is not another person with you to speak the answers. The answers will be heard inside you. Because you are alone, recognize that this will be your process. The objects of which you have asked questions will answer with their truths. These truths will resonate and be heard inside your mind and heart.

Real listening is hearing. We must be prepared and open-minded to really listen. Your willingness to listen will bear fruit: you will hear answers.

Answers may sound like this: "I have always used that." "I know where this came from." "That is not necessary." "I love that!" "Someone needs this more than I do." "That has to stay." "I know I'll never use that." "This is too large for the space." "There is too much here." "That is the only thing I really need." "I am not at peace when I look at that." "That is not functional anymore." "I know I must change this space."

Answers will come to you as long as you are willing to listen. Answers will be repeated as often as you reflect and ask.

You may feel vulnerable as you enter and commit to this phase of evaluation. It is not always easy to be still and quiet. You may be afraid to hear answers; what you hear may require you to act. You may feel unable to respond to what you hear. But remember, the truth that lives in this space and is connected to these objects is one with which you are intimately familiar.

You know this place. You own these things.

You will not feel overwhelmed with the answers you are listening for, but enlightened. Reassure yourself that you can choose to act and respond to these answers in a manner that will be comfortable for you. You have much to gain by listening; you will be able to transform this space with the knowledge you acquire. Knowledge comes in the form of answers. It will be important for you to be still and quiet to hear these insights as they come.

As you listen, feel free and unencumbered. Empty your mind of all present thoughts, and wait for new information. In this quiet place, you must trust that you will hear. You will gain the knowledge you are seeking.

Again, listening is an action. There is a reverence you will feel as you proceed, a quiet respect for knowledge and truth.

Feel grateful to be able to listen. Feel your heart beating, your breath flowing, and your senses attuned. Listening takes all of you to accomplish. As you have sought through asking, so you will receive through listening. You cannot evaluate without listening.

SimpleSpaces require that you hear.

Now that you have chosen to listen, you will realize you are beginning to hear. Audible thoughts will enter your mind: words, phrases, and ideas. Information will come containing insights pertaining to the questions you have asked of the space. You will hear simple statements, commentary, and conclusions about specific pieces and objects. This information will flow to you and through you. As you hear what you have been listening for, you must fulfill this next phase.

This phase is experienced hand-in-hand with listening: receiving.

■　　■　　■　　■

What does it mean to receive? Can a person listen and not receive? Why is receiving so important?

To receive, a person must accept, grasp, take in, or take possession of something. In this phase of evaluation, you are receiving answers.

Have you ever prepared and given a gift to someone that you feel did not accept your offering? It may have been placed in their hands, but innately you knew they did not receive. As a consequence, you did not experience as much joy in giving.

Contrast that to a time you gave a gift that was whole-heartedly received. Think about the fulfillment you experienced as a result. When a gift is received, there is much to celebrate; both the giver and the recipient are edified. Many things can be given as gifts: objects, affection, kind words. The reception of these gestures makes them gifts.

Now in this space, as you are listening for answers and insights, think about how you can receive. The knowledge you gain will be a gift to you.

Receiving is an active process like listening. To receive, you will hear and then acknowledge the hearing. You will give a place for the information in your mind and heart. You will accept the truth of these answers by allowing them to reside in you, contemplating and pondering what you have heard.

To reject an answer after hearing it, we would close our minds. To not receive what is given, we would cut off the flow of information, or abruptly disagree with what we have received. We reject a new insight by justifying an original point of view that contradicts the new insight being given. We must be open and willing to receive; we must be honest about what we hear.

Having observed and asked, we must now listen and receive.

■   ■   ■   ■

All that resides in your space has a relationship to you. It is imperative that you recognize what is necessary and vital. SimpleSpaces are free spaces. To achieve this freedom you must be willing to receive, as new truth, the answers that flow to you from the space.

This is the ultimate act of ownership: owning the answers you receive after you have asked.

Remember, in this phase of observe and ask, you questioned the purposefulness of the space. You asked to know about the objects residing in the area, their vitality and functionality. To receive, you will listen and accept as new truth the insights you hear. As you receive this new truth, you will be strengthened. The strength you gain by receiving will enable you to act: you will have the ability to transform your space, however small or great the transformation.

You will be able to create SimpleSpaces.

If we reject these truths as they flow to us, the power to transform will be diminished. Our strength to make changes will fade. We will remain with our space as it exists, and with the energy therein, whether stifled, congested, dark, overwhelmed, depressed, or just stagnant. The new energy that wants to thrive in this space will not be invited; we will have closed the door. The process of evaluation will be thwarted until it is forged anew another day.

To receive is to accept and act.

If you can find the inner strength to receive the truth, your spaces will change forever.

Feel gratitude to be able to learn this process.

Take a breath in and out. Relax. You are fulfilling this phase of evaluation in patience.

You have listened and received. The gift of insight has been given. You naturally will enter the next phase on your path toward SimpleSpaces.

Record and verify.

Step 1

I now hear and accept.

listen and receive

Step 1

evaluate

observe and ask

listen and receive

record and verify

visualize and dream

Step 1

record and verify

Inside the space, you have observed and asked, listened and received. When you feel you have received all that has naturally flowed into your mind and heart, it will be time for you to leave. Now you will move to a neutral location. This can be a favorite chair or table. You may use a computer or paper.

Now you will begin this next phase: record and verify.

All the insights you have received are registered in your mind, and have made an impression on you. Now you will want to write these impressions down.

Writing is an act of verifying something or making it real. When we write and record, we are actualizing our thoughts and feelings. This is a powerful process. As you write, you will explore anew the insights you have received about your space. You will make a record of this newfound knowledge so that you will not forget.

As mentioned, you may use a computer to record, but handwritten words are sometimes more effective and personal as they flow directly from your hand to paper.

To begin, write the name of the space you have evaluated at the top of your document. This record does not need to be perfect. It can flow in the form of words, thoughts, streams of consciousness, or mental images. It can be structured in the form of lists, phrases, incomplete sentences, or drawings.

Your objective is to record what you have observed and learned.

As you received answers about the space, you probably felt emotions connected to these answers; it is important to remember your feelings. Within these insights were truths that made you feel. Now you will want to record these truths and sentiments. Once you have written your insights, you will have received them twice: in your mind and heart, and on paper.

Try to remain alone as you accomplish this task.

This phase will take time, but not any longer than the time you have already invested in the evaluation process. You will not want to rush this record-making. Remember, writing gives you another opportunity to be honest about the insights you have received. You will want to record the truth, even if that truth seems less than positive.

■   ■   ■   ■

Now you will proceed by remembering what it was like to enter the space and stand in the threshold. Record your impressions about this experience. Record what you learned from asking questions. Write the knowledge you received, and what you felt as you received it. If you remain still and quiet while recording, you will receive the insights again.

Your observations may include statements like this: "I have realized the room is dark." "I haven't used that for some time." "The area was filled with things I have been storing." "I didn't know all that was under there." "Looking at that made me cry." "I remember when I bought that." "There is no empty space in the room." "I must find a way to change this place." "My grandmother gave that to me when I was five." "How have I accumulated so much?" "I realize what I need this area to be."

As you record impressions, be completely truthful: "I love my space, but it could be so much more." "I felt totally enervated looking in there." "I feel excited when I think of cleaning out that room!" These observations reflect the reality of how you feel about the space. This reality is what you will hold to, and honor, as you proceed.

Recording the truth will allow you to progress.

Once you have made a record, you will never lose what has been felt, learned, or understood. It is recorded. Writing your insights down has afforded you another benefit; they have become real.

■   ■   ■   ■

To verify something, we prove it is true: we attest, authenticate, or certify that piece of information. You are verifying what you have heard and felt by writing and making a record. This written record will, in very deed, make your insights real. This writing will become your new truth.

If it is truth to you, it is real.

You know what you have heard. By making a record and verifying your truth, you will be able to fulfill what that truth requires. Every space has specific requirements to be simple and free. You will find these requirements written in your record. Your insights may feel ordinary, but the truth about your space is not.

In the future, you will take other steps in the creation of SimpleSpaces. You will utilize this record and its verities as you proceed; you will always be able to remember this writing and refer to it as a guide. Protect this record, and do not lose it.

Feel gratitude to be able to write, to record and verify. This has taken time, but ultimately your SimpleSpace will give you time in return. When you feel you have written all that is necessary concerning this place, you will be prepared to continue with your evaluation. Now you will return to the space.

It is time to visualize and dream.

Step 1

I now write and make it real.

record and verify

Step 1

evaluate

observe and ask

listen and receive

record and verify

visualize and dream

■   ■   ■   ■

Step 1

visualize and dream

In this phase of evaluation, you will find time to imagine. With your record in hand, return to the room and look inside.

Now you will visualize and dream.

You have taken time to understand the realities of this space. Now is the time to visualize and dream about what this place can be.

You are still in the thinking phase. You are evaluating what the possibilities can be for this area and visualizing them in your mind. You will not touch anything or move to reconfigure it; only look, and mentally create pictures.

Using the knowledge you now have, imagine how the space could be transformed.

As you visualize and create mental pictures, project these pictured possibilities into the space. You will conceive of, and envision, a variety of spatial changes in your mind's eye. You can use colors, shapes, and pieces to change what presently exists; let your imagination take over. Visualize a space on top of the space you see. Make changes that are in accordance with the new truths you have received. This place will be transformed in your mind.

This should feel creative and free.

You can visualize at any time: the same day you began your process, or a different time altogether. You made a record that will remind you of your insights. If you can accomplish this phase on the heels of the other three phases of evaluation, it will be most effective in creating SimpleSpaces. However, you may enter the area many times until you have fully visualized and pictured all that is possible.

As you stand here, appreciate your ability to do so. Relish the opportunity you have found to be alone, visualizing. Recognize where you are in the evaluation process.

As you picture options, remember your responsibility to use the answers you have received. Your newly written record and its verities will help you visualize accurately what you want this place to be. If you recorded that it felt congested and dark, picture it cleansed and filled with light. Visualize what you think the space can become.

There is no perfect way to do this. Be patient, and trust that your visualizations will be the right thing for this place.

To create SimpleSpaces, you must have vision.

■   ■   ■   ■

Few elements may change in this area. On the other hand, this may be a space that is completely transformed. Remain true to your record.

As you visualize, your pictures will begin to expand.

Now it is time to dream.

To dream is to be carried away in your mind to a place of creating. Your hopes and desires for life and the future reside in this space inside your mind. It is a place farther away than where you visualize. Dreaming is a process more powerful than visualizing.

When we visualize, we remember our present reality and involve it in our imagining.

Dreaming goes beyond the truth of your space into an area of infinite possibilities, none of which may include your present reality or the new truths you have received. If you could create a space of your choosing, what would you dream?

When we dream, we leave our current situation, and we idealize about new possibilities. There is a hunger in dreaming that involves our heart. We dive into a pool of inventing, creating ideas in a mental space deeper than where we visualize. If we allow ourselves to dream, we will enter a realm of uninhibited imagining.

Dreaming opens our world to what-ifs, coulds, wants, and wishes.

Dreams filter down into daily life like water on a dry lawn. Blades of grass stand and grow in the sun; mercifully, water rains down, seeping in between individual blades. A parched area can find life and sustenance through the hope that dreaming affords. A dream can be living water to a space that is dry and empty. To dream is to believe in a better way, a better day ahead; a place where the sun shines, but there is no drought; where the rain falls, but there is no flood. Dreaming takes you to that place.

As you visualize your space, and what it is asking to be, allow yourself to dream. Remember, you will not be able to dream forever; reality always calls. The truth that resides here will bring you back. Life's energy will require you to engage in daily tasks.

Dream anyway.

Trust your ability to imagine. As you allow yourself to dream, you also allow the possibility that your dreams may become reality. Your dreams may trickle down.

Dreams supported by effort and commitment can come true. If we dream, but do not labor, our dreams stay out of reach. Diligence and discipline allow our dreams to become a reality. You must believe in your ability to imagine what can be. Then you must act and labor to change and influence the present space to allow room for your dreams. Do not be surprised by your imaginings, but identify and respect them.

If you fulfill all that is required to create SimpleSpaces, your dreams can become reality.

Your hopes for this space will rain down.

You have observed and asked, listened and received; you have recorded and verified. Now you have taken time to visualize and dream. Evaluation is complete for this space. You have fulfilled in patience the first Step.

Take a moment to breathe and relax. Feel gratitude for the ability to visualize and dream. It is a gift to imagine what could be. Now take the time to record these wants and wishes.

SimpleSpaces require time to think and be honest.

When you are ready, you will take the next Step.

Step 1

I now picture and imagine.

Step 1

evaluate

observe and ask

listen and receive

record and verify

visualize and dream

Step 1

evaluate

it has been a time for honesty

SimpleSpaces

■   ■   ■   ■

Step 2

eliminate

eliminate

eliminate

orange assists in cleansing

orange is the color for courage

eliminate

orange is decongestive

orange assists in cleansing

orange is the color for courage

eliminate

Step 2

eliminate

I will move forward with courage and understanding.
I do not fear change.

Step 2

I have held on too long to what I never needed.
As I learn to let go, I have all I ever want.

must it leave?

begin with a plan

decisions to make

what is sacred?

Step 2

must it leave?

Now you know the reality of your space.

You have not rejected the truth that came, but received it willingly. Having evaluated, you know your space desires newness of life. It wants to be vital. You have visualized what this might look like, but are not ready to change the area. There are natural Steps that must be taken in order for SimpleSpaces to be effectual.

Elimination is the next Step.

What is elimination? Why is it necessary in the creation of SimpleSpaces? To eliminate is to remove or discard, dispose of, or disqualify. It is to take out or omit. To change a space, you will begin by removing all that is not useful or necessary.

This phase of elimination takes courage.

You have lived with the things in this space for some time. Your eyes are accustomed to seeing them. You have walked around, slept near, and moved among all the objects in this place; they are familiar to you.

Now you will begin Step 2 by removing all that isn't needed, everything you've held onto for a future day that never comes, leaving only what is vital and useful for your journey.

Elimination is a powerfully effective process.

■   ■   ■   ■

You may ask: "Why wouldn't I begin to change the space by adding things or bringing things in?" To answer this, think of your own body.

Your body is alive. All its parts and pieces are necessary. These vital components enable you to live moment by moment, day by day. You nourish your body by taking into it the things you need to keep it alive. You could not take things in, or add things to your body, if an equally important function did not take place: elimination.

After you have ingested, a natural process of digestion begins: your body accepts what it has been given. Next, a process of absorption takes place to utilize the needed nutrients. Once the value has been derived from these consumables, your body instinctively eliminates what it can no longer use. Each of us owns a body. We are intimately familiar with this process. We do not fear elimination, but welcome and expect it. We know we cannot store all that we have put inside; we know we would die if nothing left us. We actually experience sickness when elimination is erratic or incomplete.

Homes are like bodies. They are living entities. They have parts and pieces that make them unique and complete.

All people call a space home, whatever that space may be. Some homespaces are small, consisting of one or two rooms; others are vast configurations of multiple spaces. There are people who dwell on the water, others on mountain tops. Some people have no space to call home, but roam from place to place, living in temporary enclosures for shelter from the elements.

Still others lose their homes to circumstances beyond their control.

However temporary, whatever place in which we find ourselves, wherever we feed, clothe, and shelter ourselves; this is home. As you care for your body, keeping it alive and vibrant, so must you care for your homespace. To ensure this place remains vital, you must regularly eliminate all that is not useful.

If you consumed a delicious piece of fruit, deciding to take it into your body, you would not want it to stay with you forever. The process of consuming it would be pleasurable, but you cannot hold onto it; you know it cannot stay. It will remain only as long as your body needs it; then naturally, you will eliminate. You will not fear or mourn this departure, but will understand and support your body's ability to do so. This is how you keep your body healthy and alive.

Again, our houses are the same. They are living entities. Some objects and pieces stay with us longer than others, but all should be able to be eliminated when their usefulness is gone. For many this is challenging. Their spaces are congested and constipated. The life energy that once thrived and inhabited the space has long since left; the flow of life has ceased.

Life's energy has a flow, a rhythm, or pattern.

It is marked by entrances and exits, ins and outs. These patterns are repeated hourly, daily. We are awake, we sleep, and we awaken again. This rhythm is evident in nature; all animals and plants repeat these patterns, and engage in life's energy. Water responds to this pulse; it flows, ebbs or recedes, and it flows again. It rains; the water lifts, and it rains again. This pattern is experienced, moment by moment, as you breathe in, exhale out, and breathe in again. This repetition is the essence of living.

This rhythm is the beat of life.

When we prepare a healthy meal, and are fed by consuming it, we do not stop there; the meal is eliminated, and we must, if we are to live, prepare and consume another. We bathe and are cleansed; living makes us dirty, and we must bathe again. Done, undone, and done again; a continual pattern of living. This is what our life on earth is like if we are to be healthy and endure the challenges that come to us all. No one can pass through this life without engaging in these patterns. Once we accept this reality, and embrace it, we will welcome life's energy.

If we can apply this rhythm to our homespaces, they will always resound with vitality. We will be supported within their walls and given all we need to fulfill another day.

We will feel this healthy pulse.

Energy inside a space is visible and tangible. Spaces that are frozen to life's flow are felt by all who enter. The objects residing inside may be beautiful, costly, or otherwise valuable, but if the life flow has ceased in that space, it is, in reality, no longer breathing. There are no ins and outs; life's rhythm has ceased. You have witnessed this before as you have entered certain spaces. You have felt this negative, stalled energy, this void.

Remember, we carry things into our homes to use them; we derive assistance and pleasure from them. When we can no longer benefit from their presence in the space, we must carry them out.

■　　■　　■　　■

For some people, the process of elimination is arduous, and the need to eliminate arguable. They easily bring things inside, but once inside, it all becomes necessary and sacred. Some people feel that if it was carried into the space, it must be honored and held; they become attached to their possessions. They cannot see their spaces becoming crowded and congested. Instead of purging the area, they continue to consume and fill the vessel. They sense a lack of energy, and further attempt to enliven the space by acquiring and adding new objects. Without elimination, this effort to rejuvenate is futile.

Finally, the space sits stagnant and still; the life flow has ceased. It is, in reality, dead.

When that person leaves their space forever, someone else will become responsible to eliminate and cleanse the area, a final and all-consuming process. This is almost always overwhelming for those responsible to be stewards of the newly-inherited space.

Often, people fear they will not have what they need if their spaces are free and clear. They hoard objects. Since all objects serve some purpose, they feel the need to house everything, rationalizing that they eventually will use it all. Sometimes people feel wasteful when they let useful pieces leave the space.

Some people unknowingly hide in the confusion and distraction that complex spaces provide. They may fear time to think. They feel unable to change or simplify their spaces; they feel unable to begin the process. Still others are slothful, and will not find the time or courage to eliminate what they no longer use or want. It is always a task for another day, or for another person to fulfill. Others feel too busy to engage in elimination.

Some objects have sentimental value. We honor these, and the memories associated with them, by holding onto the objects today. Many things serve as symbols of the dreams we once had. These are difficult to carry out. We feel we actually carry the dream out with the object. There are projects to be completed, pants to be worn, hobbies to be mastered, and trips to be taken. We believe that as long as the objects stay with us, so does the desire to accomplish these objectives.

To find the courage to eliminate and keep our spaces vital, we must evaluate and be honest about our present reality. What do you really use, want, hold, love, or dream about doing today? What do you have the time to do? What do you really do?

When you are able to let something leave that is not being used, is broken, or is not cherished, you open the space up for something new to enter. This may require you to live with a vacant area for a time. Allow the emptiness. When you are afraid to let an object go because you fear you will not receive another, and you keep it held in the space, you will not receive what you really want: new and necessary pieces.

■　　■　　■　　■

When people share spaces, one person naturally assumes the role of a gatekeeper. They attempt to make decisions about what to do with all that enters. When men and women live together, women usually assume this role. Every person living in the space brings things inside. It is the responsibility of each person to find the proper place for their objects, to give them a home, and then, when those things are no longer functional, to carry them back out.

Remember, our spaces can provide all we need if we are true to what we really need today.

Considering future needs, you may even own spaces, holding places, that will store things for future use. If you have evaluated, you will know what is vital and necessary for today and tomorrow's today. You will know what to store, and what to eliminate, if you have been honest. Knowledge and insights concerning future needs will be heard in the mind and heart.

Tomorrow will take care of itself if you can receive the truth of today.

When you leave this space for the last time, your arms will be empty. You came with nothing, and it is certain you will carry nothing out. Only your mind and heart will be filled. The knowledge you have gained and the emotions you have felt will leave with you.

What resides in your heartspace? Is your mind active and searching? What have you collected inside of you?

None of us knows when our final exit will take place, the final breath exhaled. Can you imagine how you would feel if you knew you were able to leave this life with your spaces free and clear? How prepared would you feel for your departure? How would loved ones feel about the places you have left behind?

You can create SimpleSpaces; the area you have evaluated is becoming a SimpleSpace. Elimination is the second Step you are taking. Be grateful for your ability to let things go.

Now that you understand why things must leave, you will be able to continue.

You will begin with a plan.

Step 2

I now understand why it has to go.

must it leave?

Step 2

eliminate

must it leave?

begin with a plan

decisions to make

what is sacred?

Step 2

begin with a plan

Now that you have learned why things must leave, you are ready to enter this phase of elimination.

You will begin with a plan.

This is a time for structure. You will find this structure in the appointing of a plan.

Your life is busy and scheduled. You must work, wash, travel, prepare, eat, clean, watch, read, make, say, hear, lie down, and stand up, and you must do these things day after day. How will you fit this Step of elimination into the dance of your life? The studio floor is already taken, filled with a variety of steps; intricate footwork is performed daily. You dance continuously.

Some days you may feel tired as you perform a myriad of musts and have-tos. The only time the dance floor is empty is when you are asleep. Even then, life's choreography continues inside your dreams.

To create SimpleSpaces, you must add another name to your dance card. These Steps must be fit into your schedule, or they will never be yours to dance.

But you say, "I don't dance!" Yes, you dance. Even without formal training, you are a dancer. We all dance. We move and breathe, reach an arm here, turn a head there. We travel and return, hold on and let go. Sometimes there is music playing, but often not, when only the rhythm of talking and breathing underscores our steps.

To fit elimination in, you must begin with a plan.

If you use a calendar, retrieve it. If you are not so scheduled, use a sticky note, and put it where you will see it. This plan will be your method of action, a way to proceed. This will ensure that elimination takes place. You will state your intentions and use these goals as a guide to follow. Writing this plan will formalize it and make it real.

With a plan in place, you can relax and keep moving.

To begin with a plan, you will:
- choose support
- choose to start
- choose to succeed

- choose support

Begin with a plan by choosing support. Share the process. If possible, invite a friend to join you. This support partner can be a great help. You can share observations with, and direct questions to, him or her. Ultimately, the decisions will be yours to make. Your support partner will motivate you to keep progressing and help you avoid stalling or becoming inactive.

Remember, the partner need only join you in the space to be a support. This person is there to share the process, not complete it for you. Your support partner cannot perform this Step of elimination because he or she has no ownership. Unless you name the support partner a steward of the space, he or she will be unable to do this for you. This person can offer support and strength as you proceed. Offer to reciprocate this generosity when your friend chooses to create SimpleSpaces, or repay him or her in another way.

If you do not know anyone who can do this for you, or if you choose not to have support, understand that you will have to motivate yourself to obtain results. It is possible to achieve success alone, but more fulfilling to share the process. This is one Step in the creation of SimpleSpaces where the company of another is encouraged, but not required. When using the 4 Steps in the future, you will feel better qualified to take this Step alone.

Solitude is energizing if you have chosen it.

Remember, the first time you walk this path, it is recommended that you choose support. You can choose what that support will be for you.

■ choose to start

Begin with a plan by choosing to start. Designate a day, and a block of time, dedicated to elimination in this space, and mark this day and time on your calendar or sticky note. By appointing a specific time and committing to it, your success will be certain. Choose a day that presently has few engagements scheduled. Initially, a reasonable time period to plan for will be 1-2 hours. However, this Step may take several hours or days to accomplish depending on the space you are simplifying. You may schedule future appointments as needed.

Unless there is a real emergency, honor this engagement in your schedule. Be prepared to carry out this commitment. Do not override this new schedule with any other event or activity.

Remember, if you reserve the time to fulfill this Step, it will happen.

■ choose to succeed

Begin with a plan by choosing to succeed. Predetermine how much you will accomplish by predicting, in a positive way, what your process will be. Choose to succeed by writing down optimistic goals concerning elimination in the space. This writing can be accomplished in the same journal you used to record insights during the evaluation phase. If this is your first time creating SimpleSpaces, you will want to be realistic, but positive, in setting your goals. Choose objectives that are attainable. If you cannot visualize the quantity of what may be accomplished, write goals that relate to quality. Describe your process in specific and general terms. While you may not know what lies ahead, be hopeful and plan for success.

Aspirations are realized when they are thought about and written down. Write what your success will feel like as you eliminate and purify this place.

Your writing may read like this: "On Saturday, I will begin the process of elimination. I will make a difference in this space. It may be difficult, but I'm ready. Julie is coming for support while I work. She knows how important this will be for me to make these decisions. She'll be honest with me. I know what needs to happen, and what I have to do. I will eliminate everything I do not use or love. I will examine every object. With Julie's help, I'll do it. I don't know how long this is going to take, but I'm committed. This will happen! It will feel so good to do this!"

By writing your goals, you are choosing to succeed.

■   ■   ■   ■

Now you are on your way. You have outlined three objectives to help you begin. This Step will soon be realized because you have planned for it. You have allowed this Step into your life, onto your dance floor.

Someday, the 4 Steps of SimpleSpaces will belong in your repertoire; this footwork will be familiar. These Steps are part of life's rhythm.

Eventually, you will know this routine.

Now that you have chosen to begin with a plan, you can keep dancing.

■ ■ ■ ■

Step 2

I now prepare to act.

Step 2

eliminate

must it leave?

begin with a plan

decisions to make

what is sacred?

■   ■   ■   ■

Step 2

decisions to make

Returning to the space, stand in the threshold of the room. Take a moment to review all that has transpired in this area.

You have evaluated this space. You have taken another Step, and learned why things must leave. You know elimination takes courage, and you have chosen to begin with a plan. As you enter the space again, you draw on the understanding and insights you have gained. If you have chosen to share the process, you will wait for your support partner to arrive.

Before commencing, you will need to acknowledge another important truth about the space. You will need this truth to proceed in the creation of SimpleSpaces.

This reality may change the way you continue to take this Step.

Ask yourself if the place in which you stand is shared.

A shared space is a place where another or others reside with you.

If the answer to this question is yes, then you must have stewardship rights to proceed. In shared spaces, objects belong to more than one person. In order to eliminate things from this place, you will need to communicate with, and receive verbal permission from, the shared owner(s). They must give you temporary stewardship, or the right, to handle their objects. You will need to make decisions on their behalf to accomplish this step. Children under the age of answerability cannot give you verbal permission or temporary stewardship rights. You are already a steward of their spaces.

All others you live with must be consulted.

Shared spaces are best eliminated by shared owners in cooperation with, and in support of, each other. If you cannot receive permission, and do not have an understanding with all space-sharers, you should not proceed. If you do, unpleasant consequences may follow. Without permission, you will find yourself at a temporary impasse. You will need to begin again inside spaces that belong wholly to you.

It is a sacrifice and privilege to share.

Be patient and thoughtful as you compromise your dreams for shared spaces. Be creative in finding solutions, and hopeful about the future of these communal places. People can change if they will take the Steps. Sometimes the decision to walk takes time.

We must respect the rights of others.

◼   ◼   ◼   ◼

If you have stewardship, you may proceed. When your support arrives from within or without, you may begin.

Feel excitement as you realize you are actually going to accomplish this Step of elimination. Appreciate that you have been able to honor your plan. Express gratitude to your support partner for their willingness to join you. Breathe in and exhale out.

There are three things you will want to do to prepare. With support available, you are ready to begin.

To prepare for the decisions you will make:

- review the record
- bring bags and boxes
- energize your efforts

- review the record

Prepare to make decisions by reviewing your record. Remember your insights, and the goals you have made concerning this space. Review your written record, and keep it with you.

- bring bags and boxes

Prepare to make decisions by bringing bags and boxes. Have black garbage bags, white garbage bags, and cardboard or plastic boxes available. Laundry baskets also work well as boxes. These bags and containers will serve as temporary holding places for objects as they transition from one space to another, and as you eliminate them.

- energize your efforts

Prepare to make decisions by energizing your efforts. Be well-rested and feel able-bodied. You will want to eat before you begin, and have plenty of water available. Elimination takes courage and energy. Making decisions can be an emotionally and physically exacting process.

■   ■   ■   ■

As you enter the room, armed for elimination, you will make a discovery. Confronted with all that resides here, you will realize you have decisions to make. You know the truths you have received concerning this place; you have been prepared to stand here. Now you will begin to re-examine all that you have previously evaluated.

Feel gratitude that you can take part in such an important and life-changing activity. Appreciate this space and all that you have accumulated.

To eliminate what is no longer useful or desired, you will examine each object. You will make choices and draw conclusions, make selections and resolutions. You will determine outcomes and verdicts.

In essence, you will make a decision about everything in the space.

If you cannot fulfill this Step, or if you are unable to make these decisions, then the process will be postponed, delayed. Ultimately, this Step will be left for another to perform in your stead. If you have physical or emotional challenges that prevent you from accomplishing this, seek the assistance of a support partner willing to join you in the space. You can give them stewardship rights to enter this area, and make decisions on your behalf. They can be your arms and hands.

Someone, someday, will look at and handle each object in this space. For areas to be vital, they must be cleansed. If you are able, now is the time to embrace this task.

As you proceed, recognize elimination as a sheer act of labor. Dress your body, and prepare your mind for this work. It is a time for courage. You will facilitate elimination if you can clearly understand and carry out the process. Ask a variety of questions as you proceed, but you will need to make only three decisions about the things you own.

You will decide to:
- keep
- share
- discard

If you are honest about the knowledge you have gained through evaluation, this will not be a formidable feat, only time-consuming. If you are focused and positive, open and willing, you will have the courage to make decisions.

A thorough examination will result in a thorough elimination of all that is unnecessary in the space.

As you handle each object, you will be reminded of the former questions you asked. If you know the answers you received, you can act immediately. However, you may choose to ask again. The most important question to ask: "Do I use this today?" Other questions include: "Do I love this?" "Does someone need this more than I do?" "Do I want to look at this anymore?" "How many choices do I want?" "How free do I want this place to be?" "What do I want to think about?" "How do I want to feel here?"

Variety is not always the spice of life. Sometimes it is too rich, and ruins the flavor of a simple fare. A great variety of objects inside the space can overwhelm. Too many choices can take too much time.

Decision after decision, things to . . .

- keep: place in boxes
- share: place in black garbage bags
- discard: place in white garbage bags

If you do not have bags and boxes, you may still carry out this step using what you have. This is a simple process. Simply proceed.

As you fulfill this Step of elimination, and make these decisions, refrain from cleaning. Do not fix things or decorate, only eliminate. You will see the dirt and debris left from living. You may have ideas about spatial changes and embellishing, but only perform this Step. Cleaning and beautifying will happen later.

■   ■   ■   ■

Begin by allowing as much natural light into the area as possible. Choose a starting point in the space. Handle every object, covering all areas from top to bottom, from ceiling to floor as you work your way around the room. Handle things on shelves, from one side to the other; inside pieces, under furniture, and on the walls. Touch everything in your path, removing each object from its resting place. As you hold each object, make a decision about it, and place it in its designated box or bag.

Keep your record available to write down any ideas or notes about needed items or repairs.

- keep

Objects to keep will be placed in boxes. These will need to be sorted and grouped according to likeness and type. This sorting will allow you to see what, and how much, you have accumulated. Carry these objects outside the space for categorizing. It will be important for you to view these objects away from this area. This will allow you to see things in a new light. You may decide differently about these things once they have been removed from their original places.

When sorting and handling the objects of another person, you may keep their things separate and available for them to make decisions about at a later time.

- share

Objects to share will be placed in black garbage bags. These black bags will conceal your objects. This will allow you to forget these things once you have made decisions about them, and continue with the process. Once these bags are filled, place them outside the room in another area. Allow these things to rest. You will know if you have made a hasty decision to share them if you are reminded of a particular object and feel real loss or regret in its departure. Try to discern what real loss is; parting with anything will feel uncomfortable.

Remember, many can use what you are not using. Carry away these bags as soon as possible. If you decide to sell these objects, you will receive money. If you decide to give these objects, you will receive in other ways. Either way, you have eliminated.

- discard

Objects to discard will be placed in white garbage bags. Carry these bags outside the space, and place them in trash receptacles as needed. Keep the area free and clear while you work.

■ ■ ■ ■

As you proceed, designate areas in the space for undecided and misplaced objects. These areas may accumulate with items as you complete this step. Make decisions regarding these undecided things as soon as possible, and place them in their designated box or bag. Take time to return misplaced items. These are things that belong to other people, and in other places. Do not postpone this task. Do not allow these piles of undecided and misplaced objects to remain.

Be true to the vision you have for this place, the dreams you have dreamed. Be courageous.

As you fulfill this Step of elimination, you will stand in temporary chaos. Allow this confusion. Allow other areas outside this space to be affected; these places will welcome the overflow. If necessary, make paths to walk through the disorder.

Invite your support partner to assist you as needed. If you are alone, resolve within yourself to stay motivated. Utilize the time you have planned for and more, but be sensitive to the schedule of your support partner and others who may need you.

Do not worry or be fearful.

You cannot make a wrong decision. You arrived without these things, and you will leave without them. You have decisions to make about what will be necessary for you to assist you on your journey.

Only you know what you need today. Press forward.

There is more to examine.

Step 2

I now choose what stays.

decisions to make

Step 2

eliminate

must it leave?

begin with a plan

decisions to make

what is sacred?

■　　■　　■　　■

Step 2

what is sacred?

Some decisions in life are easier to make than others. As you fulfill this Step of elimination, you will recognize this truth.

Some objects you handle briefly; they are easy to look at and let go. You make decisions regarding these objects effortlessly. Other objects you hold onto longer. You find it more difficult to determine the outcome of these. They seem to be a part of you, and you cannot step back far enough to get a proper look at them. Your heart is tied to these things, and they linger in your hands.

To help in this sentimental struggle, it will be important for you to realize what is sacred.

As you ponder and reflect on what is sacred, your thoughts may turn to objects that you treasure, guard, or even consider untouchable. These are things that are special to you, but are even more than special. You may keep these objects in a particular place apart from others. If danger threatened, you would protect these things, attempting to rescue them from damage or demise.

An object, though seemingly ordinary, may be considered sacred because it shared an experience with you, reminding you of a particular time, place, or event. It may honor a life lesson learned or a friendship cherished. Sacred objects may be those passed from another's life and another's hands. If an object inspires hope, generosity, or love, it may feel sacred.

When we ponder what is sacred, we think of that which is holy, hallowed, or blessed; we think of the divine, sanctified, or spiritual. Sacred things reside in a space higher than in an earthly realm.

We sacrifice for what we feel is sacred.

At this point in your process, it is important and necessary to recognize what you revere.

■   ■   ■   ■

If you look at something long enough, you will have a thought about it.

Sacred objects require reverence and acknowledgment. If all your objects were sacred, your acts of revering them would be all-consuming. If everything was believed to be sacred inside your space, you would not be able to live there. Your daily life needs comfortable and fundamentally ordinary space. As you eliminate, allow a combination of objects to remain: those that are functional and sacred.

Some things you linger with can be kept. They can be memorialized and put in a safe place. You may photograph, display, or preserve objects you feel will benefit your life and the lives of those with whom you live, even the lives of those who will enter this space after you leave. Be sure to record the necessary information about these preserved objects: dates, places, individuals, and the stories involved. You may attach this information securely to these objects so that those who handle these things in the future can benefit from their history, or you may keep this information in a separate document or journal.

Be particularly selective about the objects you save for a future day and the life energy you choose to expend in this preservation process. As sacred objects feel so to you, others may not share this sentiment. People may not understand an object's meaning once it is inside their own space. Objects passed down to another may become burdens; the new owner may struggle to honor and preserve these objects out of respect for the former owner. Extra care and attention will be given to things that are bequeathed by hands that share the same blood. This is a responsibility that the heirs of your objects may feel for the rest of their lives. Be certain about what is sacred, and selective about what you choose to pass on to others.

If we want others to feel what we have felt, experience what we have experienced, a written record can describe our life's journey to others, taking people where we went, sharing what we treasured. A written record or journal can be easily passed down; thoughts, experiences, and lessons learned can be preserved on paper and left behind. This record can share the life we lived in a personal and powerful way. Journals are sacred and of great worth; they tell the stories that objects cannot.

You have lived, whether you hold physical evidence of that life or not. Your possessions do not define you. Give yourself permission to revere an object, linger with it, and then release it, letting it go. Yesterday's dreams and yesterday's objects may not serve today's realities. You may choose to hold onto a few sacred reminders of your past. There is much to be learned from what happened before, but you will not forget who you are or where you came from if your spaces are free of memorabilia. You will actualize your selfhood by creating spaces that are free, spaces that allow you to be who you are and who you dream of becoming today.

Free spaces are not inherently free, but are bought with a price. Who will labor for you to have free space? How can you purchase this freedom? As you commit to this Step, you will realize that elimination is the act of laboring for free space. How sacred is this endeavor?

This free space will be worth more than you can imagine. You are opening the area to receive new life. Remember, as long as you hold an object in the space, you deprive yourself of other options. As soon as unused, unnecessary, or unloved objects are removed, the area becomes available for new things. These new things will come to you through friends, family, or your own ingenuity. Life continually offers gifts, but they cannot be received until you let go of what lies stagnant.

Learn to trust in this process of renewal, this cycle of reception.

What you cannot see, you will not think about. How free do you want your thoughts to be? What price would you pay for mental freedom? If your space is free, you will be free from the responsibility of thinking about the objects that once shared this place with you. How sacred would that freedom feel?

You will care for what you keep. Caring is an action, actions take time, and time is sacred. What do you want to care for in the sacred time you have been given?

After decades of consuming and acquiring, we now crave the absence of things. We crave simplicity: quiet places and empty spaces. Do not be afraid of quiet places and empty spaces; you need a certain amount of empty space to thrive, to think about your life. These spaces will not feel empty, but will be filled with life's energy. These are vibrant places that will reflect who you are today. Be courageous as you purge this area. Breathe life into this place by allowing ins and outs. Your spaces may feel emptier, but will be replete with all that is necessary, functional, and sacred.

Less is more when it is all you need. You will have all you need if you are true to what you really need today. As you realize what is sacred, you will know what needs to stay.

■   ■   ■   ■

This process may take three hours or ten, one day or two. You are not concerned; you have come prepared to labor. The objects in this space must support your life's purpose. If they don't aid you in your journey, eliminate them. If the memories surrounding an object are too painful and hold you to the past, remove it from your view. The less affinity you have for these things, even those you deem divine, the more fully you will be able to accomplish this Step and be free.

When you have emptied the space and your objects have each been handled; when decisions have been made and you have realized what is sacred, be still and rest. As you stand in the space and look around, you will see remnants of the place you once knew. Things may feel chaotic and out-of-order. You will see changes you have intentionally made to take this Step. The space will feel vacant, except for the pieces you have allowed to remain in boxes to keep.

As you view this area, you can feel it waiting. There is still a labor to be performed, a final elimination that must be accomplished. Now the dirt must leave. You must clean this place. When your energy is renewed, you will continue.

You have identified what is sacred, and made decisions about what to eliminate. Now you must remove the soil. You will clear away all signs of the former life lived: filth, trash, dust, lint, smudges, fingerprints, and stains. You will prepare this area for the next Step. Take time to repair holes and fill in gaps, wash windows and wipe walls; retouch paint, clean light fixtures, remove carpet spots, and replace faulty hardware. Eliminate all evidence of the previous place and its prior purpose. Feel free to move furniture to do this, and use whatever cleaning equipment and supplies you have available. This is a sacred act: preparing the space to be a new place.

Ultimately, you are preparing for a final departure when you will leave all this behind. Sometimes we must leave all we own while we are still living. Could you walk away from your homespace today? Would your treasures leave with you? Would life's energy bring things to you again? What do you reverence on your journey?

You have realized what is necessary and sacred; you are eliminating what you know is not. You are creating a SimpleSpace.

For now, rest and renew, take a breath and relax. Feel grateful you have had the strength to accomplish this Step.

It has been a time for courage.

Step 2

I now realize what I cherish.

what is sacred?

Step 2

eliminate

must it leave?

begin with a plan

decisions to make

what is sacred?

Step 2

eliminate

it has been a time for courage

SimpleSpaces

Step 3

employ

employ

employ

green stabilizes

green brings balance

employ

green engenders healing

green stabilizes

green brings balance

employ

Step 3

employ

I will create a space that serves today.
I do not fear labor.

Step 3

I have traveled quite a distance to come full circle.
As I create patterns of order, I walk in paths of freedom.

finding solutions

creating systems

fulfilling fundamentals

exploring possibilities

■ ■ ■ ■

Step 3

finding solutions

You have taken time to evaluate, honoring the truth you received. You have eliminated all that is not necessary or sacred, all evidence of the previous place. Now your space is waiting. You must stay on the path and keep traveling. It is time to take Step 3.

It is time to employ.

In the employ phase, your spaces will become ordered and functional. You will find solutions, create systems, fulfill fundamentals, and explore possibilities. By eliminating objects that could leave, you have kept only objects that must remain. Now this space desires a new structure and form, a redefining of purpose.

What does it mean to employ?

To employ is to make use of, engage, or enlist the help of something. You are going to employ, or make use of, solutions and systems to create order. You will employ the fundamentals of living, and find time to engage in exploring possibilities. By enlisting the help of objects in the space, you will create a place that is functional and true.

In Step 3, you will establish patterns. Following these patterns in your life will lead you to walk in paths of comfort and safety, allowing you to live more efficiently. These patterns of living will bring peace. Your space will become a place of peace; there will be definition, boundaries, and structure. With these elements of order present, you will feel something enter the area.

To employ is to usher in freedom.

As you employ what your space needs, it will be transformed. This will require patience as you first find solutions. It is a time for searching.

■   ■   ■   ■

Today is a new day. You can feel pleased with your efforts. You have watched as the space has changed. You have been honest about the truth you received, and have fulfilled the Step of elimination in patience.

Now the space is quiet, clean, and ready.

White garbage bags have been carried out and placed in trash receptacles. Black garbage bags have been held until you have felt certain about the decisions you have made. Undecided objects have each been handled, and you have traveled to return misplaced things to their proper homes.

The remaining objects rest in boxes. These have been sorted, grouped, and left alone. You have chosen these objects to remain with you, and they wait to be reordered. Will they return to the place you found them or be utilized in a new way? The choices are numerous. These things are vital, and their use will be ensured. For now, you aren't sure what to make of this disorder.

How are you going to realize your visions for this space?

As you stand here, it may feel unsettling to see things in such disarray. If you can stay in this place of confusion a while longer, you will have the time you need to find solutions.

Every space has its own characteristics, attributes that are unique. It is defined by size, shape, and form. Every space serves a function, fulfilling a specific need or a variety of needs. A space will more easily realize its designated purpose if it is focused and defined.

Originally, you decided on a use for this space. It may have been given a name: the living room. You created its function, and integrated it into your daily life. You have become intimately familiar with this area; you have cared for it. This place has served you, and you have served this place, perpetuating its intended purpose. You have honored what you asked it to be, and it has remained true to its name.

Early on you recognized a truth: this space is not perfect. For every strength and positive attribute, it also had a flaw or shortcoming. You discovered these limitations by living with the space. You learned to work around and with these weaknesses: "I like this, but that isn't so good." "It is a nice room, but the windows are small and don't let in enough light." "There are plenty of shelves, but they aren't deep enough." "I love the room, but this piece only fits against that wall." You learned to live with these imperfections; you continued on in spite of them.

As you look into this area, remember what purpose it has served. You have completed the Step of evaluation, being honest about the truth. You have eliminated, leaving only the vital and sacred. Now you are left with a bare and vulnerable place; you can see the flaws inherent in this space.

To remain true to the vision you have had for this area, you must admit the weaknesses that exist here.

These problems have always afflicted this space. Now you must confront them. The place is emptier, and the problems remain. How can you transform this area and create what you have dreamt about without addressing these weaknesses? You can pretend they don't exist, cover them up, or decorate over them. You can stop and put things back where they were. You may say: "It wasn't really so bad. It worked." But somewhere inside, you know what you have visualized for this space; you can still see it in your mind's eye.

Vision is what motivated you to be courageous and labor. You carried out objects you have held a long time. You accomplished this to realize your dreams for this space. It was a time for wishes, and you made more than one. Now, you may feel to reconsider. Confronted with the weaknesses you have always known, you may feel inclined to stop moving; you may not want to take another Step. The choice will be yours. You can always choose your actions. Feel gratitude to be able to see weaknesses. Appreciate the strength required to admit what isn't perfect.

Take a breath and exhale.

To find solutions, you must admit imperfections, acknowledge what you want, and then wait to receive.

To find solutions, you must acknowledge:
- weaknesses
- wishes
- waiting

- weaknesses
Acknowledge the weaknesses of a space. This will enable you to be honest and introspective as you recognize your need for solutions.

- wishes
Acknowledge your wishes for the space. This will enable you to ask for what you want. You will have identified and expressed the desires of your heart.

- waiting
Acknowledge the waiting required to find solutions. This will enable you to be patient and receive answers when they come to you.

■   ■   ■   ■

Solutions will always come. You must be quiet to hear them. You will recognize them as solutions because they will sound sensible. These answers may be something you never considered; they may feel new to you.

If an area has always felt crowded, and you have eliminated what you do not use, solve this congestion and bring order by moving a larger piece to a different space altogether. The piece was useful, but not necessary in this place. If an area has served many functions, but has always felt disjointed, redefine it. Now, it will serve a single function. The solution was found in simplifying its many purposes to create one.

Some spaces require few solutions. Some may need to be cleansed and employed for an original purpose. Do not search for solutions when the existing purpose is sufficient. However, do not settle for, or acquiesce to, the weaknesses of a space either. Have hope and seek answers; trust your instincts as you search. SimpleSpaces can be created in any area. Only you know what the truth requires.

Solving challenges in one area may concurrently affect other areas. Be prepared for this. Expect it. Be patient with the chaos and turmoil this will create. You are choosing disorder temporarily. You will create order lastingly. Take the time you need to acknowledge weaknesses, express your wishes, and wait for answers. Take time to find peace.

■   ■   ■   ■

Finding solutions will breathe new energy into this place. Ultimately, life's energy will permeate all the spaces you call home. You must pass through the confusion and disarray to realize the peace and harmony that can exist.

You will always find solutions if you take the time.

When you have found an answer, accept it gratefully. This answer will bring change. Be willing to employ this solution. You may need to move, shift, transfer, relocate, or reposition objects in the space.

Finding solutions will uplift you.

You are creating a SimpleSpace. There is always an answer.

There is always hope.

Step 3

I now search for answers.

finding solutions

Step 3

employ

finding solutions

creating systems

fulfilling fundamentals

exploring possibilities

Step 3

creating systems

Now you know there is a solution, a way to create the vital energy that wants to reside. You have had hope and searched. You have acknowledged weaknesses and challenges, recognizing that no place is perfect. Your goal has been to create a SimpleSpace that is perfectly true. To progress further, you will continue to employ.

Now you will create systems.

A system is a plan that works for you. It is a method, practice, or course of action. It is a routine, strategy, or way of operating.

Systems are comprised of parts that function together.

Our body is a system made up of systems. These operate independent of one another, but in harmony, to maintain life and health.

Homes are systems and likewise contain systems. Systems can be seen in kitchens, bathrooms, bedrooms, laundry rooms, closets, playrooms, family rooms, sheds, storage rooms, living rooms, entryways, dining rooms, pantries, attics, porches, and offices.

Systems exist in every space.

In a kitchen, there are many objects: utensils, dishes, and cookware. To create systems, we will utilize these items, strategically placing them inside the space. We may use containers to serve as holding places for these objects. We will place these containers in visible or hidden locations in the space. We are creating a system that will involve the use of these things.

This system will create a pattern in the space. This pattern will create a path. We will follow this pathway as we walk, move, and care for daily needs.

If we are successful, we will know where objects are, and rely on this knowledge. We will be able to reach without thinking, retrieve without searching, and walk without wandering. A system that has been successfully created and employed will allow us to fulfill needs in a timely manner. We will establish a pattern, walk a path, and accomplish a life task.

Effective systems are intentionally created, and integrated into our life's journey. These patterns create new paths to follow. We understand why and where we are going. We walk these pathways willingly.

Ineffective systems are those that are haphazardly, unintentionally, or falsely created.

If you moved objects in your kitchen into new holding places, you might feel immediate frustration or confusion as you search for what once had been readily available to you. This searching for essentials would waste sacred time. If you regularly put these utensils, dishes, and cookware into new places, it would regularly create disorder. Eventually, these erratic patterns would be adopted into the behaviors of those in the space; the searching for these needed objects would become part of the system and the patterns associated with it. Searching for things would be the pathway walked; the lack of an effective system would create wandering.

Dependable systems greatly affect the productivity and quality of life. We want to rely on systems. We want to accommodate the daily functions of living, moving from one task to another. If we can care for fundamental needs, then we are free to think of other things.

Our brains allow us to quickly adapt to patterns and methods, further allowing us to tend to higher levels of thought. The brain wants to rely on the routines that systems create to take care of basic needs. These routines become habits.

Think about the way you dry your body after bathing. This pattern, or way of wiping and clearing the water, is repeated shower after shower. If you were to towel off differently, and attempt to change this, you would find it uncomfortable, even difficult. We are creatures of habit. Our brains allow us to recognize patterns and create pathways. As we follow these pathways, our actions become habitual; our behaviors become routine. If we can obtain food readily, clean and clothe our bodies effectively, and sleep in a safe, warm environment regularly, then we will be able to accomplish the more intricate patterns of living.

Systems enable us to sustain life.

Now we are free to live a life that benefits others. We will be able to reach out beyond our own domain into the space of another. We will be free to interact, help, and give. This is the fruitful life, a meaningful existence. This is why we create systems: to be able to walk in paths of freedom. We must be able to depend on these methods of living to reach out beyond our own spaces into the lives of others.

■   ■   ■   ■

There are systems manifest in the outside world. When you stop at a traffic intersection, you participate in a system. Lights, wires, timing devices, and painted lines on the pavement create patterns and pathways that allow you to come and go without hurting anyone. Nature is filled with systems, all created to sustain and perpetuate plant and animal life.

The systems you employ can be simple or complex, and are semi-permanent. They will change to adapt to the needs inside the space.

A simple system would be that of hanging your bathrobe on a hook in the bedroom. You repeat this pattern of behavior because you can. You chose the location, found the appropriate component, a hook, and hung that hook to create the system. Then you used it. If you proceeded to hang many coats on the same hook, the system would no longer be functional. You would need to create a new system that accommodated multiple coats and your bathrobe.

Complex systems consist of multiple parts. These serve to manage many objects. We find complex systems in closets, toy rooms, kitchen pantries, and elsewhere. Managing many objects requires complex systems. These are still functional and efficient.

An effective system will create:

- patterns
- order
- limits

- patterns

Systems will create patterns in the space. These patterns will create pathways of repeatable behavior in the utilization of objects.

- order

Systems will create order by separating, defining, and grouping like-objects. These groupings will create definition and organization in the space.

- limits

Systems will create limits in the consumption and acquisition of objects, restricting the flow of unnecessary and extraneous things into the space.

■   ■   ■   ■

You have vital objects waiting; these things rest in boxes to keep. As your understanding grows concerning systems, you will be able to incorporate these functional and sacred pieces into new arrangements, remaining true to your vision for this place. You will create systems by positioning things. You will use containers and components as needed.

A container is a hollow shape that serves as a holding place for objects. Containers come in a variety of shapes, sizes, colors, and materials. A component is a useful object: a hook, rod, rug, various household ware, or piece of furniture. Remember, systems are semi-permanent: you will use these containers and components in different arrangements for varied periods of time. If resources allow you to purchase containers and components, purchase those that will endure and last. However, systems can be employed without buying anything; rely on what you already have. A variety of objects may be used to invent these systems. Be creative.

Placing similar objects inside containers will bring order and organization to the otherwise random placing of things in the space. Simplifying creates organization. You will manage objects easily if you have eliminated sufficiently.

Employing systems will allow you to organize things: to separate, define, and group like-objects. As you fulfill this Step, you will create a free and inherently organized place. As you simplify your spaces . . . you will free-up and organize your life.

As you create systems, remember: if you can't see it, you won't use it.

This rule of the space is realized in every facet of life. If you cannot see something, you will not think about it. If you do not think about it, you will not use it. You will choose this fate for many objects: snow boots, childhood letters, and underwear, to name a few. These things you will find when you need them. Living will remind you to use them. You will not need to put these in visible places; you will not want to see them constantly. Place these items in hidden locations.

Some objects inspire positive thoughts and productive behaviors. These things motivate you. They benefit you on your path. Place these objects in open, visible locations. Develop patterns of behavior around these things: a journal by your bed for writing; an alarm clock across the room that requires you to get up to turn it off; running shoes and exercise clothes accessible in your closet for daily use. Choose what you want to see, and be aware of, on a daily basis. Objects that motivate deserve visible locations.

It is important that every area has a certain amount of free space within it.

This is space that is empty and free of objects. When you look at this area, you are not reminded of anything. Remember, if you look at an object long enough to see it, you will have a thought about that object.

If we look, long enough to see, we will think.

Intentionally leave a surface clear, a section of the wall empty, a corner of the room vacant. Strategically place objects and pieces to create this free space. If your room is full, so will your life feel full; your thoughts will be occupied. Your mind will not be free to contemplate new subject matter, for it will be constantly stimulated by the objects you see. Inspirational trinkets will produce inspirational thoughts.

Photographs will remind you of people and places. Decorations will make you aware of how your space looks. You need a certain amount of empty space to think things that you might, may, or could think. As your body needs room to move and breathe, so your mind needs room to roam and rest. Trust that this principle of placement is true. Find solutions and create systems that allow for free space.

■   ■   ■   ■

This Step of employ takes time. Creating systems takes ingenuity and analytical thinking. If you take the time necessary, you can create systems that will be used every day.

Observe the pathways already in place. Can you create a system designed for these existing behaviors? If dirty laundry is dropped on the floor in the same spot every day, can you place a basket there to catch it? The most effective systems invented are those that use current pathways and routines in the space.

If you want to encourage different behaviors and routines, you will need to implement different systems, and establish new patterns. You can create new paths.

No one can create systems for you unless you invite someone into the space and give them temporary stewardship. There are people who will do this for you. Your support partner may be invited to assist you. However, even a professional will need to be familiar with your history and preferences to create successful systems inside your space. If you choose support in the creation of systems, accept this assistance as a gift. Do what you can to help, and be willing to learn as you watch. Sometimes we are not able to fulfill this Step alone, for a variety of reasons. But remember, you know this place; you live within these walls; you know your story and how it is told, day after day.

If possible, do not dread this phase of SimpleSpaces or feel overwhelmed. Feel gratitude for the ability to analyze and devise systems.

Take a breath in and out. Relax. You are creating a perfectly imperfect system that will be perfect for you.

Remember the visions and dreams you have had for this place. If needed, refer to your written record.

Begin by allowing as much natural light into the area as possible. You will start by moving larger pieces into position. This is easy to do now that the space is free and clear. Bring the boxes, with objects you are keeping, into the area. These boxes, or box of objects, should be sorted and grouped according to likeness and type. You will create order by giving these necessary and sacred things new homes. These new homes, or holding places, will allow you to use all that you have chosen to keep.

Having found solutions for the weaknesses that exist here, you will now create systems. You will put vital things back into motion. These systems will allow your solutions for this place to be realized. Your dreams for this space will come true.

You will do three things to create a system:
- imagine
- implement
- initiate

- imagine

Create a system by imagining the placement of your vital objects in the space. These things need new homes. Picture these things inside containers and components if needed. Measure the areas inside the space, and write these tabulations on paper. Measure your containers and components, and mentally check that they will fit inside the desired configurations you are seeing. You may visualize your system several different ways. Refer often to the objects needing to be housed. These may include: jeans waiting to be stacked in a closet; framed photographs needing to be displayed on a flat surface; books wanting to be placed on a shelf. These are things for which you are finding new homes. They will now take part in a system you are creating and employing. Imagine this system placed in the space.

Ask yourself: "Will I be able to use these objects here?" "Is this system going to create patterns I can live with every day?" "Will it create pathways I can follow?" "Do the objects in this system need to be visible or hidden?" "Will this system become a habit for me to use?" "Will it make my life easier?" "Will it feel natural to reach for these things?" "Who will use this system?" Ask these questions now while you are visualizing.

Imagining systems will make it possible for you to create them.

Remember, your systems will be employed as you stack the jeans, display the photographs, or place the books. These systems will consist of parts working together to create a whole: your jeans will take part in a closet system; the photographs will become part of a tabletop arrangement; your books will be included in a shelf scheme. You will use different sizes of containers and components as needed to employ these systems. You may use clear, shallow bins in which to stack the jeans, a smooth surface for the photographs, or a variety of baskets to house the books.

Before you can create systems, you must first imagine them in the space.

■ implement

Create a system by implementing it. Place, arrange, position, hang, fold, put away, set aside, and put inside all the objects that belong in this space. Now you will apply all that you have imagined. You will make your system a reality. You are creating new homes for these things. Remember what you have envisioned as you implement your system.

Use the measurements on your paper to help guide you in the placement of containers and components. Put the clear bin, filled with jeans, on the closet shelf. Arrange the photographs on top of the table. Position the basket of books on the bookcase shelf.

Ask yourself: "Does this system belong here?" "Am I creating a simple or complex system?" "Do these objects need containers?" "How many containers do I really need?" "Now that I can see this system, does it make sense?" "Have I employed a system that will allow me to use what I am keeping?" "Will I really use these things for which I am finding new homes?" Ask these questions as you position your objects and create the system.

Implementing a system will allow you to make your visualization a reality; all you have imagined will now be brought to pass. You may try several different configurations as you create these patterns in the space. This process of trial and error is necessary. Rearrange things until it feels right.

Implement your system by bringing it to life in the space.

■ initiate

Create a system by initiating it. Test the efficiency of your system by beginning to use it in your daily life. There is a time when you will say: "This system has been created." Now you will begin to use it. Let time pass as you live with these patterns in the space. Allow pathways to be established as you put into practice the system you have imagined and implemented.

Begin to use the jeans in the clear, shallow bin on the closet shelf. Notice how the photographs look on the table. Reach for a book inside the basket on the bookcase shelf.

Ask yourself: "Does this system work?" "Do I reach for these things easily?" "Do I repeat this pattern of behavior?" "Are the objects I have housed in this system really vital and sacred?" "Will I use this system without thinking?" "Do I want to see these things every day?" Beginning to use your system will allow you to evaluate its effectiveness, and re-evaluate the necessity of the objects you are housing. Continue to eliminate as needed.

Initiate your system by using it.

When a system doesn't work, you will know it. You will not be able to integrate the new pattern into your life. You will not repeat behaviors that the new system encourages. Pathways will not be followed. Objects will not naturally find their way back into holding places.

Eventually, you will reject this method, and begin to create a new system. This is a natural process, and it will actually teach you valuable lessons about the patterns of living that already exist in the space. Embrace these failed methods. It is the same as with other ventures, like cooking; you don't know how salty a recipe should be until you have added too much.

Creating systems will be an ongoing process of trial, error, and success.

When you choose to employ systems, you will invite order. Peace will follow. Those who share your spaces will benefit from and feel this harmony. Properly placed systems will ease, and can eliminate, much of the frustration experienced in searching for an object, or remembering where it was last seen. You can create an arrangement that provides a place for everything and allows everything to be in a place.

This can be more than a dream or wish.

This is the reality of a SimpleSpace.

If you choose not to create a system at this time, one will be created anyway. It may be unstable or haphazardly placed, but you will witness the evidence of it in your daily life. We must have reliable patterns to fulfill our journey, paths of order to follow to sustain basic needs. These wait for your hand to bring them into existence. Recognize the opportunity you have to transform this area.

Do not live in fear of failure. Dwell in a place of forgiveness and fortitude.

You are creating a SimpleSpace.

If you can invent systems, you will invite peace.

Step 3

I now establish patterns.

creating systems

Step 3

employ

finding solutions

creating systems

fulfilling fundamentals

exploring possibilities

■　■　■　■

Step 3

fulfilling fundamentals

You have taken time to understand the weaknesses of this space. You feel positive about the solutions you have found. Chosen objects have been positioned in systems, creating new patterns. You need these things, and follow pathways to use them. You remembered this rule of the space: if I can't see it, I won't use it. You applied this rule as you implemented new arrangements. This Step of employ has taken time and energy, but has been exciting and fruitful. You sense calmness in the space.

There is order here.

Now you will enter the next phase of employ: fulfilling fundamentals.

As you live inside this newly ordered space, you acclimate yourself to the pathways that have been created. You incorporate new behaviors into your life's dance, your daily routine. Now you begin to use the bathrobe on the hook in the bedroom; the alarm clock across the room that requires you to leave the bed to turn it off.

You have eliminated what is not useful for your life today. As you stand inside the space, you spend less time in decision-making. You have given yourself fewer choices, but you don't feel anything lacking; this is an abundant place. The Steps have created a true space.

Solutions have brought hope. Systems have brought order. This phase of employ will bring its own understanding of what must be done. Now, you will employ a new plan. This plan will involve your behavior. Now that you have ordered the space, you will bring order to your actions.

You will fulfill fundamentals.

The fundamentals of living are those functions related to the basics. They are the essential aspects of daily living, elementary and foundational. The fundamentals in life are those activities and processes that are indispensable, necessary, and primal.

When you think of what is fundamental in life, you think of those activities that must be engaged in to sustain life. You must eat, drink, clothe your body, sleep, have shelter, tend to relationships, and develop a trade or skill as a means to provide the basics. These fundamental needs must be met in order to sustain and perpetuate life. There are many other activities and pursuits we may want to explore. These higher attainments may include: gaining an education, developing talents, engaging in service-oriented activities, pursuing artistic and creative endeavors. Unless you can accomplish the basic or essential needs of living, you cannot pursue the higher attainments.

Not all people standing on the earth today are pursuing higher levels of living. They spend most of their journey meeting basic needs. These efforts occupy their lifespaces, and will be fulfilling because they sustain life. They will realize the fruit of their labor: food, shelter, and clothing.

Other people stand in different places, born into families and spaces that encourage them to pursue a variety of life's activities. With their basic needs met, they can concentrate on reading, writing, thinking, analyzing, drawing, swimming, painting, singing, dancing, playing, theorizing, healing, and many other interests. They are able to meet the basic needs of life, and still engage in other pursuits. They can weave both fundamental and experiential threads into the fabric of their lives. There is joy in satisfying basic needs, and joy in loftier ventures. If we are healthy in mind and body, and we stand in fortunate spaces, we will be able to pursue all levels of living.

No matter where we stand, we must first fulfill fundamentals.

This phase of employ will allow you to focus your mind on taking care of the basics. This is not to the exclusion of other activities; rather, it is to understand and adhere to this rule of the space: if you fulfill fundamentals first, all other pursuits may be accomplished in their time. Likewise, if you fail to provide for the fundamentals of life first, you will not have the true freedom and focused energy necessary to pursue higher aspirations.

Fulfilling fundamentals means doing today what you know must be done to sustain life, and doing it first. Trust that as you do this, other dreams will be realized.

■   ■   ■   ■

When you wake up in the morning, you begin the day by fulfilling several universal functions. These are described as universal because all human beings must engage in these. You will eliminate bodily wastes and fluids that have accumulated while you slept. You will clean and dress your body. You will ingest food and water. Interspersed in these basic functions are a variety of activities that are unique and individual. You may choose to: read, write, meditate, pray, watch, fix, clean, play, run, drive, call, arrange, perform, swim, create, uplift, purchase, hold, or grow. Our functions are as varied as our capabilities, resources, and motivations.

Pause to think about your days.

How do they flow? What are your life patterns? How do you intersperse the fundamentals of living with higher aspirations? How do you feel about your life? How do you spend the time you have? On what plot of ground do you stand? Who stands with you? Is it shared space, or do you stand alone? Can you stand? If you share your spaces, what are your feelings towards those with whom you live? Are you grateful you can sustain life?

Do you receive all that life offers you?

All people experience life's rhythm: we do, it is undone, and we do again. We speak, it is forgotten, and we speak again. We clean, it is soiled, and we clean again.

In the midst of these patterns, this relentless flow, we must find the time to be. We must understand the basics, and why they ask to be held and embraced first, but we must be true to who we are in the process.

As you fulfill fundamentals:

Can you smile and look, hope and dream?

Can you laugh and listen, lift up and reach out?

Can you stop and remain, be quiet, be still?

Who comes to your aid, knocks on your door?

Who visits your space, shares your life?

Who's a friend, a foe, a stranger, a neighbor?

What happened before, after, during, or since?

Do you drive fast; sing soft, laugh loud, sleep long?

Do you advance or retreat, pursue or revert?

Do you blame, accuse, condemn or lambaste?

Are you the most, the least, the best, the worst?

Who asks you, heard you, called you, or knew?

What is above you, below you, beside or within?

Can you observe and ask, listen and receive?

Your journey is a series of actions performed in a linear pattern. From the first to the last, you move and do, until you fall asleep because you can do no longer. One action follows another, each taking its moment on stage. Although you may engage in many activities in a given day, only one at a time is fulfilled. Then you sleep, which is an active process itself.

As time passes, this line or chain of events gently arcs, reaching for its start, reaching for the point of origin in its path. Finding that place in space, it attaches, and the arc becomes a circle.

A cycle is born.

This cycle or circle of events contains your sequence of life's activities; it turns around and around. With each revolution, time is marked. Moments become minutes, hours, and days, evolving into weeks, months, and years. A calendar shows you this evidence. Your life passes. The rising sun marks the start of the daily cycle, and then sets at dusk as the moon and stars take their place in the sky. Sleep is the welcome respite for all. You open your eyes, and light fills the space.

You begin again.

Each day you choose, if you are in a place to choose, between must-dos and want-tos. What a privilege and responsibility it is to have choices. A rule of the space is realized: if you fulfill what must be done, you will find time for what wants to be done. If you fulfill fundamentals first, you will obey a natural law. This law dictates that you must sustain life before you can create it. Complying with this law will bring freedom.

Now you are free to live your life.

■ ■ ■ ■

As you live and fulfill fundamentals, are you able to sustain your emotional life with the same activities that sustain your physical life? Are you able to care for your body and soul? Are these parts of you separate? As you consider basics, consider the needs of your entire being: your body and mind, your physical and emotional self.

Consider your heart and soul. Your soul is the wholeness of you. Your heart lies in the center of all you do.

You have internal spaces that make up who you are. These are sacred places that overlap and overlay, allowing you to be, to think, and to do. Fulfilling fundamentals will sustain all these parts as the whole of you. When you care for the body, you care for the physical self, but not the physical only. Your emotional self is sustained as well, and strengthened and enabled to continue its role in supporting your journey. Ultimately, fulfilling fundamentals will sustain all your spaces, and give you the freedom to be nurtured on a higher plane, with a healthier diet, in a wider circle of enriching activities. Fulfill what must be done, and you will find it was what needed to be done, wanted to be done.

Now what can be done waits for you.

If you share your life with others, and if your arms hold offspring, efforts to maintain the essentials of life will be interspersed with helping these others to fulfill their fundamentals. Only you will know when you have completed the basics of living. Only you will know what you and your offspring need to thrive. These basics are activities that must be accomplished to sustain vitality, the life energy of the body and soul, your physical and emotional self.

You will recognize the fundamentals because fulfilling them feels familiar. Fulfilling them may even feel like drudgery, and you may want to put them off. You may think that if you could do something more interesting or creative first, you would feel motivated to get the basics done later. However, your efforts at creativity will not be whole-hearted, for your energy will be diffused by the lack of truth resounding in your spaces, a lack of truth born by postponing the basics.

Your entire being knows on a deep level that life must be sustained today. Your spaces require this reality to survive. If you postpone the fundamentals, even for a few hours, the truth that exists in the space will be affected. In futility, you will attempt a project here, or an appointment there, but you know in your mind and heart that the fundamentals await you. This division of energy thwarts productivity and peace.

If you can accomplish the fundamentals first, you will enliven your lifespaces for other endeavors; you will be free to live.

Real freedom requires discipline.

Some will not trust this principle. They may rationalize: "I get around to the basics. They always wait for me!" Although this may be true, a greater truth prevails: while the fundamentals wait, so does the real freedom to create. Real freedom requires you to be true to this order, to honor this truth. Your spaces are ordered. Can your actions be?

■   ■   ■   ■

There may be times when your life is filled with obligations to others. Remember, before you can assist another, you must first sustain yourself. You may experience sickness or debilitating injury. Fulfilling fundamentals may be more than you can do, all you can aspire to accomplish. Even the basics may seem overwhelming. Accept these limitations. Strive to feel gratitude for whatever you experience, knowing you gain wisdom and compassion from trials and troubles.

When you are able, you will accomplish the essentials. You will be strengthened by your efforts to live, supported by spaces within and without. Life's patterns will cycle around. A season of higher creativity will wait for you.

Be strong, and take hold of the discipline that is required to fulfill fundamentals. Newly ordered spaces require a new way of living.

Choose to walk in paths of freedom.

Step 3

I now sustain life first.

Step 3

employ

finding solutions

creating systems

fulfilling fundamentals

exploring possibilities

■ ■ ■ ■

Step 3

e x p l o r i n g p o s s i b i l i t i e s

Solutions have been found, and systems created. New patterns have emerged that have brought order into the space. By fulfilling fundamentals, you have also ordered your behavior. You have accomplished the basics needed to sustain life first. This has allowed you to pursue higher activities with full purpose of heart. Truth resounds in your spaces, those outside you and within. Now you are free.

You are free to explore possibilities.

This phase of employ is necessary. You have established order. To create a place of peace, you will need to do something more.

You began the creation of SimpleSpaces by choosing to walk. You took the first Step: evaluate. Standing in the threshold of your chosen space, you observed and asked, listened and received. You found solitude, and used paper and pen to record and verify all you had received and felt. Returning to the space, you lingered for a time as you visualized and dreamt about all that this area could be. You did not dismiss your dreams, but gave place for them in your mind and heart. Time passed as evaluation was fulfilled in patience. You embraced this thinking phase, and were completely honest with yourself.

The time came for moving, and you took the second Step: eliminate. You recognized the courage needed to fulfill this Step. You learned why things must leave. You decided to begin with a plan so that this cleansing would come to pass. As you returned with bags and containers, you recognized there would be decisions to make. To assist in this effort, you considered the question: what is sacred? This determination allowed you to keep what was necessary and cherished; you eliminated all that was not useful or revered. An emptier and imbalanced place remained.

To bring order, you continued by taking the third Step: employ. You needed to find solutions and create systems to set these vital pieces back into motion and restore balance. These systems created patterns, and from the patterns, pathways emerged. You followed these paths daily. As you committed to fulfill fundamentals first, your behavior became ordered. Following pathways did not weigh you down or stifle your energy, but allowed you to be creative. Self-discipline afforded you the ability to walk in freedom.

In this final phase of employ, you will add the finishing touches. Now, you will explore possibilities. You will decorate. Your SimpleSpace will make itself known. It is a time for beautifying.

■　　■　　■　　■

To explore possibilities, you will consider the potential and promise of this space. You have dreamt about this place. It has been ordered, but what else does it need? Asking this question will open your mind to many possibilities. To complete this Step of employ, follow these guidelines.

To explore possibilities, remember:
■ function first
■ give gifts
■ respect resources

As you employ functionality and creativity within the boundaries of available resources, your SimpleSpace will manifest itself.

■ function first

To explore possibilities, remember function first. If a space is functional, it is fashionable. If it works for you, it is going to be simply beautiful. A functional space includes purposeful pieces and objects. Now is the time for you to add these elements.

If your homespace has no entryway closet, hang a row of durable and decorative hooks. You may not want to see coats and bags hanging there, but the functionality of this option creates its own aesthetic. This system will be used every day, and you will appreciate this solution over and over. Make sure your space realizes its potential by allowing it first to be functional.

There is a visible integrity in areas that assist and serve. Style cannot fully accomplish this. If an area is to resonate with energy and vitality, the objects within it must have a purpose beyond mere decoration. Some pieces may only create a picture, but if most of the items in your space are beautiful and functional, you will be dually benefited. True spaces serve true purposes in life. Align the elements in this area to accomplish this result.

Remember function first. The present systems you have employed will easily adapt to and receive these changes.

■ give gifts

To explore possibilities, remember to give gifts. What can you offer this space? You may give imagination and creativity. When you give of yourself, you will receive in return. To know what gifts to bestow, you must ask: "What can I do to enrich this place?" "It is ordered, but what can I do for it now?" Whatever you give will be received. The space will be touched and made complete by your hands.

Can you add color to the walls? Does this area crave a living element? What textures are felt here? Could you make something unique for this space that cannot be replicated? What singular refinement can you now provide? What bright and vibrant thing can you add? The most enduring and beautiful spaces are created by the personal touch of the giver. The most cherished offerings are gifts of self.

Your space will receive these gestures, and joy will be returned. Every time you visit this place, you will be reminded of and edified by the unique gifts you have given. This will be a place of peace because you have invested in it; you have given time, talent, and heart.

To fully explore possibilities, remember to give gifts.

■ respect resources

To explore possibilities, and venture into this phase of creativity, remember to respect resources. Whatever riches, fortunes, or support you have in reserve, be honest about that supply. A vital space resounds with truth. The objects living inside are necessary, and have been carefully selected. You must honor the reality of your resources as you bring things into this space. If you can afford to add something, you may. These additions will truly beautify if you choose elements within the truth of your available resources. When you spend what you do not have to design or decorate, this falsehood, likewise, will be reflected in the area.

There is an inseparable connection between your own truth and the truth of your spaces.

Falsely accumulated objects are those you cannot afford or do not truly need; they do not belong to you, or you did not receive them honestly. These will send negative energy into the area. You can create beauty with only one piece if that piece belongs wholeheartedly to you. A SimpleSpace is free . . . free from holding to the past or predicting the future. It is also free from falsehoods and pride.

Respect resources as you explore possibilities.

■   ■   ■   ■

This is your final endeavor to employ. It has been a time to beautify, a time for creativity. You have considered all this area needs to be complete. It has been evaluated, eliminated, and now employed. You have fulfilled in patience your ability to explore possibilities, remembering to think function first, give gifts, and respect resources.

Now it is time to leave the space. You will let it be.

It is a perfectly imperfect place that resounds with truth. It has been touched by your hands. You've labored to breathe life's energy into this area, giving all you can.

Your SimpleSpace has been born.

Step 4 awaits.

Step 3

I now give to the space.

Step 3

employ

finding solutions

creating systems

fulfilling fundamentals

exploring possibilities

Step 3

employ

it has been a time for order

SimpleSpaces

Step 4

enjoy

enjoy

blue is calming

enjoy

blue strengthens the inner core

blue is calming

enjoy

blue brings serenity

blue strengthens the inner core

blue is calming

a time for peace

enjoy

Step 4

e n j o y

I will return the space to a place of peace.
I do not fear the quiet.

Step 4

All I have done or hoped to be exists in the space that I call me.
As I have labored, I have realized my place of peace.

the fruit of labor

live in joy

what is cleaning?

this is serenity

Step 4

the fruit of labor

You take the fourth Step of SimpleSpaces into a place of your creating. The walls are protective; the flooring is sure. Objects and pieces have been arranged. This is your space. There is room here for all you need, including others whom you will invite. There is ample light. There are appealing colors, and a variety of shapes and textures. Your hands have held each object; only the vital and sacred remain.

As you enter this area, your breath flows freely in and out. There is truth here, realized through honest evaluation and elimination. You employed a plan that would work. You have labored, allowing life's energy to be seen and felt.

This space is not stagnant; it is peaceful and serene. It is quiet, but alive. You know this place of peace cannot last forever. It will continue to move and change, but for now it is perfect in a truthful, honest way. It is perfectly imperfect, and you accept it fully. You embrace what you've created, and what has become.

It is today . . . a time for reaping, a time to enjoy. It's what's left for you to do.

You must pick the fruit before it falls.

This Step of enjoy marks a time to reap what you have sown; to realize the fruit of your labor.

There is always a fruit from labor, from living. Work produces a product. If it is thoughtful, purposeful work, it will prepare fertile ground for planting, and yield a bountiful harvest. If we avoid the labor of living, we will still produce a fruit, but it will be bland and tasteless. It may appear beautiful on the outside, but inside it will be full of powder and mush.

Labor cleanses and strengthens, stretches and tests. We realize what we are capable of when we labor. We understand our limitations, and expand our abilities. But as we labor, we cannot forget why we work: to produce fruit.

There will come a day when we must reap what we have sown. If we do not reap, our fruits will not be gleaned; they will die on the branches. If we wait a moment too long to reap, the ripened fruit we've produced may fall to the ground. When we finally stop to gather, it may be bruised and taste rotten.

With our eyes wide open, we must recognize when our time to reap has begun. We must cease laboring long enough to realize the fruit of the harvest, the result of our efforts.

Labor will always produce for us what we have purposefully sought.

■   ■   ■   ■

Work is the tool we use to create. Life is a series of workings: you harvest what you have planted, and reap what you have sown. What you put in, you take out. What you invest in, you profit from. What you send out comes back to you.

To live, we must do. When we stop doing, we die. Then, there are no more dones and undones, ins and outs. As long as you can aspire and respire, you will continue to produce fruit. When you stop breathing, you will finally rest. Then, no labor can be performed.

We will all experience a moment when respiration ceases. This is part of the journey. This is the door we must all pass through to leave the space. Let us not invite that moment before its appointed time. Let us remember to stop working only long enough to enjoy the fruit of our labor.

Your space has been revived and breathes fresh air. It is returning to you what you gave to it. As you have labored in this place, now you must realize and glean the fruit. Recognize the season you have entered.

You have stepped into enjoy . . . a time to reap.

Pick the fruit before it falls.

Step 4

I now recognize my efforts.

the fruit of labor

Step 4

enjoy

the fruit of labor

live in joy

what is cleaning?

this is serenity

Step 4

live in joy

You picked the fruit while it hung from the branches. It was whole and unblemished. You recognized the time to reap, and didn't wait a moment too long. This is the fruit of your labor.

What is this fruit?

As you bite into it, your mouth waters around the piece; your taste buds know what the ripening has enhanced. It is sweet, and warmed from the sun. It is good. Not only do you chew and swallow, but you enjoy yourself in the process. It is satisfying to know this fruit came from your tree. You are grateful to realize such a profitable picking.

It has been well worth the labor.

When a fruit is sweet, it signifies a worthwhile effort or labor accomplished. Naturally, you will feel happy at this signal. You have worked hard. You have been patient and disciplined as you labored for this fruit. Happiness is something you have anticipated and waited to feel; something for which you have hoped. However, there is an emotion that runs deeper than happiness. It is more desirable and lasting, sweeter to feel than happiness.

It is joy.

Once you have tasted and can recognize this fruit, you will naturally be drawn to its goodness. You will want to live in this joy. This is the essence of Step 4, enjoy: to literally live in joy. As you held the warm fruit, so you live in this contented and grateful state of happiness. It has naturally come from your labors performed. You cannot turn it away.

The space has been prepared for the flower of joy to bloom.

■   ■   ■   ■

You have employed systems, and created patterns of living. These patterns have in turn created less of frustration, contention, and searching. Objects rest in holding places available for use. There is enough free space and time for introspection and relating. There are paths of order to follow that lead where you want and need to go.

You live in joy in this space, above all else.

You know joy because you know her sisters: heartache and despair. These have been in the space, and they may return. Once admitted and momentarily embraced, they do not stay long. This is a healthy and balanced place, and their presence won't affect that balance. They are ushered out when they've had their say. You won't ignore their presence; this will only lengthen their stay. In time they will leave, and joy will call you again.

This place is real, and freely allows all your emotions to reside within.

In this space, you have what you need, and you use what you have. You feel complete. There is less of wanting, scheming, or finding a way to acquire what you never needed before. This is a joyful place in which to be.

You are content.

As you live in joy and enjoy this place, you sense a gift emerging, a favor appearing. In the quiet, you sense an ability to walk away. You realize you are free to leave. You are free to venture away from this sanctuary. You have invested time here, laboring. Now your investment returns. Reach out to receive what your space now wants to give.

This gift is freedom.

This gift affords you the ability to visit other places: to serve, associate, learn, and produce, away from this area. You are free to leave, and take your joy with you wherever you go. Other spaces need you, and you are openly invited and able to depart.

When you return to this space, you will find it as you left it. There may be objects out of their holding places, but peace will still reside; vitality will still resonate. Life's energy breathes here. Your systems will bring order again and again.

All who inhabit this space will be sustained as they follow these paths, and remember what is sacred. They too will taste the sweetness of this fruit. They will be able to live in joy, and share this joy with others.

■   ■   ■   ■

Step 4 has shown you the fruit of your labor. It is sweet. This place is ordered and real. Your SimpleSpace has given back to you the gifts you bestowed. Now you are free to leave, and take joy with you wherever you go.

As you have simplified this space . . . you have freed-up your life.

It is a time for rejoicing.

Today, you live in joy.

Step 4

I now receive the gift.

Step 4

enjoy

the fruit of labor

live in joy

what is cleaning?

this is serenity

Step 4

what is cleaning?

Living happens in spaces large and small. Your SimpleSpace provides all you need to successfully traverse the terrain of your journey. You have created this place by choosing vital objects. They have been placed in containers, and incorporated into systems to help you use them. This created patterns of behavior that you have repeated naturally; pathways you have walked willingly. You have been given a gift in the space: you are free to leave, and accomplish tasks in the world outside this haven.

Because of your labor, you have realized a fruit that is wholly good and delicious. You live in joy in this SimpleSpace. Other emotions cycle through, but joy stays with you longer. You enjoy this phase, and long to have it last.

As you have passed through Steps 1, 2, and 3 in this process, you wonder if Step 4 will be transitory. Will you leave this phase, in time, as you have the others? How can you linger here and enjoy longer?

How can you make this Step last?

When you ceased your labors, and began to pick the fruit, you recognized the timing. You had worked inside the space; instinctively, you knew it was time to harvest. You knew a fruit had developed, and was now available for you to reap and enjoy. You gathered it before it fell to the ground, and just in time. As labor had a season, reaping the fruit, harvesting, had a season as well.

You realized this: there is a time when you must pick the ripened fruit on a tree until the last piece is harvested and enjoyed. Then the pleasure of reaping will have its season. Eventually, the fruit of that tree will be gone. The tree will stand bare.

You can leave your space, and venture into someone else's orchard to enjoy their fruit, but you know it doesn't really belong to you; it isn't as sweet to eat. You must return to the space to accept the reality of your own season. You must recognize when there is no longer fruit to eat. You will live in joy until then.

Can this season of joy be lengthened? The answer is yes.

To enjoy this phase longer, to extend this season of reaping, remember this rule: to enjoy longer, you must return the space to a place of peace.

You must clean.

This is not difficult. You already follow daily patterns that sustain your systems and perpetuate order. You realized a moment in time when this space rested, perfectly imperfect. You recognized this moment after you had explored possibilities, and given all you could. You stepped back, and knew your labored place had become a SimpleSpace.

As you live inside, vital energy permeates the area. You come, go, and come again; cook, consume, and cook again. You choose to create chaos, retrieving objects from their holding places. You use these things to make projects, give gifts, and complete tasks. This chaos is necessary, and your space supports the effort. You know that when the project is complete, you must clean the space. It is a time for returning, a time for restoring. You will return the space to a peaceful place, and it takes only minutes. The result is restoration.

You will restore what once was.

To experience restoration, you must handle each object, and return each to its original home. You will revisit your systems, retracing the steps initially used to retrieve these things. You will recognize patterns, and walk the paths that have allowed you to find these objects, carrying in your hands the pieces you have used.

Travel directly to these holding places. Do not delay, or create intermediate resting spots for these objects. Order your behavior by returning the space to a place of peace now. The sooner you restore what once was, the sooner you will be free.

Your space craves its newfound balance. Truth, peace, and vitality want to resonate here. Your objects are to be used, but must be returned to their original places in order to reclaim this peace. All who share the space with you will need to be true to this principle; they also must follow this rule of the space to be able to live in joy longer.

What is cleaning? Cleaning is the act of returning a space to a place of peace. Cleaning is the act of restoration.

■   ■   ■   ■

After objects are returned to their holding places, the remaining soil must be carried away as well. Clear surfaces and free spaces make the removal of dirt easy. Only vital objects reside here, and you will easily dust, wipe, sweep, vacuum, scrub, rinse, disinfect, and purify these areas. Life's energy creates the need to clean. We do, and it is undone; we wash, and it is soiled. Life's energy calls us to task.

When we recognize that cleaning is an energizing process, a life-generating practice, we will embrace this activity. These well-ordered spaces will look and feel cleaner longer, even when the evidences of living are present. Quiet places and empty spaces feel cleaner than congested and stagnant areas.

Life's rhythm flows and is continuous, but you can experience what is sacred by returning the space to a place of peace.

Immediately, you will feel the area become aligned and balanced. Every object is in a place, and there is a place for every object. Your mind will unwind, and your thoughts will be lucid. You can enjoy this space longer, and live in joy another day. It has been a time for returning.

To restore the space, to clean this place, there are three guidelines. Three rules of returning:
- sustain systems
- perfect pathways
- control chaos

Following these guidelines will help you understand what cleaning is, and enable you to enjoy longer.

■ sustain systems

To return the space to a peaceful place, to clean, you must sustain the systems you have employed. You must be willing to continually test the efficiency of your systems, making sure they are functional. Ask yourself: "Are my systems working, and being used daily?" "Am I able to return objects to their holding places within these systems naturally?" Feel free to make changes to your systems as you live with them.

To clean effectively and restore what once was, be wary of what is being carried into the space. Ask yourself: "Is this object vital, and can it be implemented into my existing systems?" "Do I want this?" "To whom does this object belong?" "If this stays, can I or its owner carry something else away?"

To sustain systems, remember this rule: for every object carried into the space, another must be carried out. This will maintain balance, and lengthen the lifespan of your systems. Following this law of balance ensures that ins and outs happen.

To clean, you must sustain systems.

■ perfect pathways

To return the space to a peaceful place, you must perfect pathways. These paths have come from the patterns that emerged when you created your systems. You use these paths to return objects to their resting and holding places. You walk many paths each day within your space. Observe the existing patterns being lived, and the pathways you follow.

Ask yourself: "Are these pathways natural?" "Do I follow these paths daily to fulfill basic needs?" "Do my paths save time and energy?" "Am I wandering as I return objects to their holding places?" "Do I feel lost and confused in the space as I am returning things?" "Are others in the space adapting to these patterns?" "Can they follow these paths to fulfill their fundamentals?" "Do these patterns simplify life, and encourage productive and efficient behaviors?"

Perfect pathways as you experience them. Be aware of how you are traveling as you clean the space. Make sure your paths are clear and unobstructed. You must know where you are going to create a place of peace.

To clean, you must perfect pathways.

■ control chaos

To return the space to a peaceful place, you must control chaos. Choose the chaos you need to accomplish the projects you desire, and then clean the space by returning objects to their holding places as soon as possible. Allow objects to be out of place temporarily. Understand that creativity is facilitated by using the things you have. You can create what you visualize and need in life by choosing and controlling chaos.

Even quiet places and empty spaces must be visited by confusion.

However, if confusion remains, it will choke the life energy in a space. Controlling disorder will restore calmness. Remember, chaos is welcome because it doesn't stay.

To clean, you must control chaos.

■   ■   ■   ■

As you follow these guidelines, you will prolong this Step; you will live in joy longer. The fruit will be sweet and available long after you have picked it. You will be able to enjoy your SimpleSpace for an extended period as you journey.

However, there is a truth that must be accepted, another rule: when you can no longer return the space to a place of peace, it will be time to fulfill the 4 Steps of SimpleSpaces again.

There will be a day when you will leave this phase of enjoy.

Cleaning will not help you live in joy longer. Time will have passed. You may sense that the vitality of your space has diminished. Systems will seem less functional. Patterns will not be as clear. New pieces will arrive in the space that former systems cannot incorporate. You may feel overwhelmed in an area that once comforted you. Your thoughts will not flow as easily. Even as you identify these feelings, and make these observations, you are beginning the 4 Steps. You are evaluating. If you choose, you will fulfill in patience each Step again. Your life's journey expects this to happen. Life's rhythm will ask you to create SimpleSpaces, and then, in time, create them again. If you are honest, you will know when.

However, you will notice a difference this time. As you proceed, you will realize that you have become familiar with the process. This intimacy will empower you to become proficient at walking this path. What initially took much time and effort, now will happen sooner and more easily.

As you create SimpleSpaces again, you will become a master at taking these Steps.

Just as you cannot prepare one healthy meal and call cooking complete, you cannot create a SimpleSpace and be done forever. You know you cannot eat ripened fruit always. A new season of labor will be required to prepare, plow, plant, prune, weed, water, grow, and sow. You will clean, and live in joy until that season arrives. Life's energy will ask this of your spaces as long as you breathe.

Do not fear repetition. This is the essence of healthy living.

This is the beat of life.

■   ■   ■   ■

Some people try to live in joy long after they have a right to be there; they ignore the absence of ripened fruit to eat. They pretend all is well in their orchard. Their spaces crave a diligent hand, a willing worker and steward, but none is found. They who once deserved to enjoy this space, and live in joy, cannot see the signs: the time for reaping has passed. The energy of their SimpleSpace has long since lost its vibration.

All they need to do is to labor again, but unable, they stay inside the space. They stand idle and unengaged, inactive in this place. Like a houseguest that will not say good-bye long after the invitation indicated, so are those who try to live in joy without proper labor and effort. Their smiles are forced; their energy belies the truth: we must earn our stay, work our field, and pay the price to eat the fruit of the laborer.

It is true in every space.

You will live in joy until you know the time is past. Then you will need to leave. If you are a wise steward of SimpleSpaces, you will heed the signs. You will return here to enjoy after you have received an invitation, an invitation you can obtain by laboring.

For now your space is new, viable, and clean. It resonates with energy, balance, and order.

What is cleaning? Cleaning is a time for returning the space to a place of peace. Cleaning is the act of restoration. You do this willingly, and whenever it is needed.

You linger in this Step of enjoy. You have every right to feel welcome, and to stay. For now, you belong.

It is a time for serenity.

Step 4

I now make joy last.

Step 4

e n j o y

the fruit of labor

live in joy

what is cleaning?

this is serenity

■   ■   ■   ■

Step 4

this is serenity

Maybe it is day; maybe it is night. The absence of light will not change how you feel. You have accepted your truth, and you do not fear repetition. This is your life.

Your joy is subdued for a time as you experience something quite remarkable . . . serenity.

You remember the day you found this space. Time cannot remove the memories. You hear voices from long ago, faintly remembered. It was here you learned to accept the reality of entrances and exits, a time to stay, and a time to go. You watched spring shine through windows, summer heat the walls, fall decorate your eyes with color, and winter keep you inside. Snow fell. You watched.

Some things you wanted never came, but you have received what you have sought. You have lived, and time has passed; your traveling has taken many paths. You have fulfilled each act in a line, one behind another. Sleep has come with the moon; the sun has spurred you on in activity.

Many people have entered this space, old and young, friend and enemy. All have left gifts. Some people you have held and nurtured, loved and lost. Most wanted to be here with you. Some have not.

Your space has felt chaos, heard anger, and sensed heartache. It has witnessed pleadings, passions, and penitence; solitude, service, and sacrifice; forgiveness, forgery, and fortitude. It has known happiness, desire, and hope. With all it has seen and known, it has remained, its walls protective, and flooring stable. Your feet stand here, if you can stand. You are not ushered out, but allowed to stay, and try your living another day.

Your space is a mirror that reflects what resides. It remains as long as nature's hand allows it. Your living passes through, however defined, and still your space remains. Until you breathe a final out, and leave by a different door, you are welcome here.

■   ■   ■   ■

In the quiet of the day, or the stillness of night, you can make peace with your journey: to accept where you have come from, and choose where you are going. In a place deep inside, you find a spot to plant a seed of love. It grows if allowed, and powerfully fills all you have become. It colors your spaces, those outside and in, with bright light and peace. You do not dread the journey.

Someone has entered who can stay for a time, share a dream, hold your hand. Love will allow all to stand in this space. There are words never spoken, but thoughts have been realized. Truth lives. It shines in the mirror before you. It has been with you all along.

It is quiet, still, and tranquil in this space. You hear messages meant only for your ears. You feel peaceful, calm, and unperturbed. Harm's way is far, and injury, uninvited, waits for awhile. You are patient and poised. You rest from your labors, untroubled and smooth. A motive to move is brushed away as you stay. Quiet serenity bathes your heart with living water. You trust this space.

Who asks you, heard you, called you, and knew?

Who comes to your aid, comes to the door, visits your space, shares your life?

What is above, below, beside, or within?

Your life happens here; you welcome it in, and you know that serenity is a moment long. You linger to listen. A whisper calls your name.

A SimpleSpace has been born, and can never forget your life, your path, your simple breath, in and out. Your heart is full as you stand in this place; you remember, you listen, you dream. You accept where you've come from. And until it's all changed by paths crossing through, you savor the quiet. Your love has found space. It is worth any labor to rest in this place, this time of serenity.

For you this is home.

From the first to the last, you move, and you do . . . moments on stage, a continuous dance. The line gently arcs, reaching for its start, until a circle is formed. You do not fear repetition. Life's energy flows, and knows the space, this simple, true, and free place. It has called you here, and now you can hear. Now you know what your space has seen all along. When it is time, you will know when to go; a last breath spirals upward. Your space will remain. You know your home. You will never really leave.

It rains; the water lifts, and it rains again. A SimpleSpace is here.

This is serenity.

■　　■　　■　　■

Can you observe and ask, listen and receive? Can you evaluate, eliminate, employ, and enjoy, and begin again . . . and begin again?

Life's rhythm asks that this pattern remain.

If you can take the Steps, and see, you will realize your spaces all are free.

Step 4

I now find peace.

Step 4

enjoy

the fruit of labor

live in joy

what is cleaning?

this is serenity

Step 4

enjoy

SimpleSpaces

SimpleSpaces

SimpleSpaces

SimpleSpaces

SimpleSpaces

SimpleSpaces

I will always find serenity.

SimpleSpaces